COMPREHENSIVE RESEARCH
AND STUDY GUIDE

T.S. Eliot

EDITED AND WITH AN INTRODUCTION
BY HAROLD BLOOM

CURRENTLY AVAILABLE

〜〜〜

BLOOM'S MAJOR DRAMATISTS

Anton Chekhov
Henrik Ibsen
Arthur Miller
Eugene O'Neill
Shakespeare's Comedies
Shakespeare's Histories
Shakespeare's Romances
Shakespeare's Tragedies
George Bernard Shaw
Tennessee Williams
🖉

〜〜〜

BLOOM'S MAJOR NOVELISTS

Jane Austen
The Brontës
Willa Cather
Charles Dickens
William Faulkner
F. Scott Fitzgerald
Nathaniel Hawthorne
Ernest Hemingway
Toni Morrison
John Steinbeck
Mark Twain
Alice Walker
🖉

〜〜〜

BLOOM'S MAJOR SHORT STORY WRITERS

William Faulkner
F. Scott Fitzgerald
Ernest Hemingway
O. Henry
James Joyce
Herman Melville
Flannery O'Connor
Edgar Allan Poe
J. D. Salinger
John Steinbeck
Mark Twain
Eudora Welty
🖉

〜〜〜

BLOOM'S MAJOR WORLD POETS

Geoffrey Chaucer
Emily Dickinson
John Donne
T. S. Eliot
Robert Frost
Langston Hughes
John Milton
Edgar Allan Poe
Shakespeare's Poems & Sonnets
Alfred, Lord Tennyson
Walt Whitman
William Wordsworth
🖉

〜〜〜

BLOOM'S NOTES

The Adventures of Huckleberry Finn
Aeneid
The Age of Innocence
Animal Farm
The Autobiography of Malcolm X
The Awakening
Beloved
Beowulf
Billy Budd, Benito Cereno, & Bartleby the Scrivener
Brave New World
The Catcher in the Rye
Crime and Punishment
The Crucible

Death of a Salesman
A Farewell to Arms
Frankenstein
The Grapes of Wrath
Great Expectations
The Great Gatsby
Gulliver's Travels
Hamlet
Heart of Darkness & The Secret Sharer
Henry IV, Part One
I Know Why the Caged Bird Sings
Iliad
Inferno
Invisible Man
Jane Eyre
Julius Caesar

King Lear
Lord of the Flies
Macbeth
A Midsummer Night's Dream
Moby-Dick
Native Son
Nineteen Eighty-Four
Odyssey
Oedipus Plays
Of Mice and Men
The Old Man and the Sea
Othello
Paradise Lost
A Portrait of the Artist as a Young Man
The Portrait of a Lady

Pride and Prejudice
The Red Badge of Courage
Romeo and Juliet
The Scarlet Letter
Silas Marner
The Sound and the Fury
The Sun Also Rises
A Tale of Two Cities
Tess of the D'Urbervilles
Their Eyes Were Watching God
To Kill a Mockingbird
Uncle Tom's Cabin
Wuthering Heights
🖉

COMPREHENSIVE RESEARCH
AND STUDY GUIDE

T. S.
Eliot

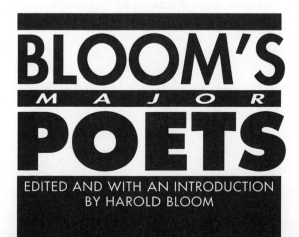

BLOOM'S *MAJOR* POETS

EDITED AND WITH AN INTRODUCTION
BY HAROLD BLOOM

3 5 7 9 8 6 4 2

ISBN: 0-7910-5109-9

Chelsea House Publishers
1974 Sproul Road, Suite 400
Broomall, PA 19008-0914

1995/16.96 9/99

Library of Congress Cataloging-in-Publication Data

T.S. Eliot / edited and with an introduction by Harold Bloom.
        p.   cm. — (Bloom's major poets)
"This volume brings together study guides to five of T.S. Eliots'
most influential poems: 'The love song of J. Alfred Prufrock,' 'La
Figlia Che Piange.' 'The Waste Land,' 'The Hollow Men,' and 'The
Journey of the Magi"—Editor's note.
        Includes bibliographical references (p.   ) and index.
        ISBN 0-7910-5109-9
        1. Eliot, T.S. (Thomas Stearns), 1888-1965—Examinations—Study
        guides. I. Bloom, Harold.   II. Series.
        PS3509.L43Z87243 1999
        821'.912—dc21   98-39703
                                                          CIP

Contributing Editor: Barbara Fischer

Contents

User's Guide

This volume is designed to present biographical, critical, and bibliographical information on the author's best-known or most important poems. Following Harold Bloom's editor's note and introduction are a detailed biography of the author, discussing major life events and important literary accomplishments. A thematic and structural analysis of each poem follows, tracing significant themes, patterns, and motifs in the work.

A selection of critical extracts, derived from previously published material from leading critics, analyzes aspects of each poem. The extracts consist of statements from the author, if available, early reviews of the work, and later evaluations up to the present. A bibliography of the author's writings (including a complete list of all books written, cowritten, edited, and translated), a list of additional books and articles on the author and the work, and an index of themes and ideas in the author's writings conclude the volume.

~

Harold Bloom is Sterling Professor of the Humanities at Yale University and Henry W. and Albert A. Berg Professor of English at the New York University Graduate School. He is the author of over 20 books and the editor of more than 30 anthologies of literary criticism.

Professor Bloom's works include *Shelley's Mythmaking* (1959), *The Visionary Company* (1961), *Blake's Apocalypse* (1963), *Yeats* (1970), *A Map of Misreading* (1975), *Kabbalah and Criticism* (1975), and *Agon: Toward a Theory of Revisionism* (1982). *The Anxiety of Influence* (1973) sets forth Professor Bloom's provocative theory of the literary relationships between the great writers and their predecessors. His most recent books include *The American Religion* (1992), *The Western Canon* (1994), *Omens of Millennium: The Gnosis of Angels, Dreams, and Resurrection* (1996), and *Shakespeare: The Invention of the Human*, 1998.

Professor Bloom earned his Ph.D. from Yale University in 1955 and has served on the Yale faculty since then. He is a 1985 MacArthur Foundation Award recipient and served as the Charles Eliot Norton Professor of Poetry at Harvard University in 1987–88. He is currently the editor of other Chelsea House series in literary criticism, including BLOOM'S NOTES, BLOOM'S MAJOR SHORT STORY WRITERS, MAJOR LITERARY CHARACTERS, MODERN CRITICAL VIEWS, MODERN CRITICAL INTERPRETATIONS, and WOMEN WRITERS OF ENGLISH AND THEIR WORKS.

Editor's Note

This volume brings together study guides to five of T. S. Eliot's most influential poems: "The Love Song of J. Alfred Prufrock," "La Figlia Che Piange," *The Waste Land*, "The Hollow Men," and "The Journey of the Magi." My introduction discusses all of these poems, with an emphasis on the true origin of Eliot's tradition in English and American Romanticism.

The critical views begin with Conrad Aiken's psychological reading of "Prufrock," accompanied by the witty excursus of Christopher Ricks on the name "J. Alfred Prufrock," as well as a commentary by Donald J. Childs on the clinical metaphors in the poem, and remarks by Lee Oser on the relevance of Eliot's Puritan heritage.

"La Figlia Che Piange," perhaps Eliot's most poignant lyric, is contextualized by F. O. Matthiessen in the fictive world of Henry James. The poem's curious mixture of memory and desire is commented on by George Williamson and David Ward, after which Ronald Bush notes the poem's emotional detachment, which I think is just barely sustained by Eliot. A psychoanalytic account, based on the work of Melanie Klein, is given by Tony Pinkney, who traces the ambivalence in Eliot's portraits of women.

The Waste Land, Eliot's central poem, somewhat differs from his own account of his relation to tradition, which is followed here by Graham Hough's strictures upon the poem's lack of unity. A Christian interpretation is ventured by Northrop Frye, a great Protestant critic. Richard Ellmann usefully analyzes Ezra Pound's editing of *The Waste Land* into its final form, while A. Walton Litz notes some of the peculiarities of Eliot's "Notes" to the poem. In a brilliant reading, Eleanor Cook categorizes Eliot as a poet of Exile, after which Cleo McNelly Kearns accurately traces *The Waste Land*'s relationship to Walt Whitman.

"The Hollow Men" is commended by Helen Gardner for its challenging difficulty, and by Hugh Kenner for its unversality. Sir Herbert Read sees the poem as happily coming before Eliot's conversion, while B. C. Southam indicates Eliot's deliberate effort to make "The Hollow Men" a Dante-esque work.

"The Journey of the Magi" is viewed by both Grover Smith and Ronald Tamplin as a poem balanced between negation and belief. Kinereth Meyer and Rachel Salmon concentrate on the reader's role in Eliot's conversionary language act. In a final judgment, James Tuttleton relates "The Journey of the Magi" to what he regards as the modern crisis of unbelief.

Introduction

HAROLD BLOOM

One can fight a long war against T. S. Eliot's criticism, and still confess a lifelong fascination with his best poems: The Waste Land, and a group that certainly includes "The Love Song of J. Alfred Prufrock," "La Figlia Che Piange," "The Hollow Men," and "The Journey of the Magi." Probably one could add "Gerontion" and "Little Gidding" to any short list of Eliot's most lasting poetry, but the five poems examined in this little volume can be called his essential achievement in verse.

The perpetual freshness of "Prufrock" is a surprise each time I return to the poem. Actually, reading "Prufrock" (preferably out loud to oneself) is never quite the experience I expect it to be. Christopher Ricks charmingly demonstrates the incongruity of "Love Song" and the outrageous name J. Alfred Prufrock, and yet this dramatic monologue remains something of a defeated erotic reverie. In his very useful Inventions of the March Hare (1996), Ricks gives us a richly annotated version of Eliot's poems of 1909–1917, and includes an unpublished passage of the "Love Song." The missing middle, "Prufrock's Pervigilium," plays in its title on the Latin poem Pervigilium Veneris (fourth century A.D.), the "Eve of Venus," which had a great vogue in the era of the splendid critic Walter Pater. Eliot had nothing good to say of Pater, probably because his own sensibility was essentially Paterian, but Prufrock seems to have read Pater's historical novel, Marius the Epicurean. Pater, the prophet of the Aesthetic movement in England, exalted perception and sensation, and deprecated dogmatic belief of any sort. Marius the Epicurean has a memorable scene in which the authorship of the Pervigilium is ascribed to Marius's dying friend, Flavian. Ricks shrewdly notes Pater's hint that Flavian's illness is venereal, and something otherwise obscure in Prufrock's dramatic monologue is illuminated when we intuit that J. Alfred's erotic timidity is allied to his obsessive fear of venereal infection.

The "Love Song" is a perpetual "dying fall," its "hundred indecisions" a series of erotic evasions. Brooding on the arms of women, which have for him an overwhelming sexual power, Prufrock will never bring any of his incipient relationships to the moment of crisis. His poem continues to pulsate with a barely repressed energy, and may be the most remarkable instance in the language of a deferred eroticism transfiguring itself into a sublime eloquence.

2

Even as a boy, I fell in love with "La Figlia Che Piange," which remains one of Eliot's incantory triumphs, and the poem he chose to conclude the volume *Prufrock and Other Observations* (1917). Eliot's weeping girl is far more intense than the alluring women of the "Love Song," but the chanter of "La Figlia" is very like Prufrock: another obsessed evader of the sexual experience. Nearly 60 years of reciting the lyric to myself have only enhanced its aura for me; few poems in the language so evoke erotic longing, the sense of an unrealized relationship.

And yet the voice of this lyric is in one respect not Prufrockian; its imaginative sympathy adheres to the weeping girl, and hardly at all to her departing lover. Something very like a Paterian privileged moment, or secularized epiphany, is being celebrated, even as the voice retreats into detachment, the autumn weather of the soul. The Paterian flesh of radiance against a darkening background is the sunlight woven in the girl's hair. Eliot, notoriously unsympathetic to John Milton's poetry, vies with Milton as the poet in English most celebratory of the erotic glory of a woman's hair.

Despite himself, Eliot always remained a high Romantic lyric poet, with profound affinities to Shelley (whom he professed to dislike) and Tennyson (to whom he condescended). Any vision of Romantic love poetry would be impoverished if it excluded "La Figlia Che Piange."

3

The Waste Land, though something less than a unified poem, is Eliot's masterwork, by common agreement. Where few agree is on the question as to just what *The Waste Land* is doing, as a poetic performance. Is it a lament for Western cultural decline, for a Europe in retreat from Christianity? Or is it a very American elegy for the self, in direct descent from Walt Whitman's magnificent "When Lilacs

Last in the Dooryard Bloom'd." Clearly the second, I would insist, though mine remains a minority view.

Eliot's own "Notes" to *The Waste Land* are frequently outrageous, never more so than when they explicate the song of the hermit-thrush by remarking, "Its 'water-dripping song' is justly celebrated." Why yes, particularly when the hermit-thrush sings its Song of Death in Whitman's "Lilacs" elegy. Ostensibly mourning the martyred Lincoln, "Lilacs" more pervasively both celebrates and laments the Whitmanian poetic self. Eliot's poethood, and not Western civilization, is the elegiac center of *The Waste Land*. Personal breakdown is the poem's true subject, shrewdly masked as the decline and fall of Christian culture in post-World War I Europe.

Such a judgment, on my part, hardly renders *The Waste Land* a less interesting or aesthetically eminent poem (or series of poems, or fragments). Hardly an escape from either emotion or from personality, *The Waste Land*, three quarters of a century after its publication, seems a monument to the emotional despair of a highly individual Romantic personality, one in full continuity with Shelley, Tennyson, and Whitman, who are far closer to the poem than are Eliot's chosen precursors: Dante, Baudelaire, Jules Laforgue.

Northrop Frye followed Eliot himself in reading *The Waste Land* as a poem of Christian redemption. I think that Eleanor Cook is more accurate in her subtle emphasis upon the poem as a representation of exile and of private grief. No one is saved in *The Waste Land*, any more than Lincoln or Whitman is saved in "When Lilacs Last in the Dooryard Bloom'd." Both grand elegies for the self are American songs of death, including the death-in-life of poetic crisis.

4

"The Hollow Men" (1925) is the culmination of early (and major) Eliot, a grim and permanent achievement, indeed a parodic masterpiece. Though the chant is overtly Dantesque, I hear in it Shakespeare's Brutus of *Julius Caesar*, a drama replete with "hollow" Roman patriots, who protest their endless sincerity, only to be subtly exposed by the playwright. Brutus, no Hamlet, but dominated by a Macbeth-like proleptic imagination, kills himself, still blind to his own hollowness. Eliot, who perhaps unconsciously was more affected by *Julius Caesar* than his beloved *Coriolanus*, parodies saints as well as "patriots." The power of "The Hollow Men" is its universality. Though some critics interpret the poem as a portrait of a world without belief, waiting for the return of Christian revelation, scarecrows hardly seem candidates for any redemption. Eliot himself was moving towards conversion (two years later, in 1927) but nothing in "The Hollow Men" intimates that such movement is possible.

Eliot's poetry of belief—in "Ash Wednesday," "The Rock," and *Four Quartets*—seems to me considerably less persuasive than his visions of the waste land. "The Journey of the Magi" is Eliot's most effective "religious" poem because its speaker dramatizes the poignance of exile, always Eliot's true mode. The Magus speaks for Eliot the poet, and not for Eliot the Anglo-Catholic. Like Tennyson, whom Eliot had praised for the quality of his doubt, the Magus stands between two worlds, never to be at home in either. At his best, the poet Eliot remained dispersed. ✿

Biography of
T. S. Eliot

(1888–1965)

Thomas Stearns Eliot was born on September 26, 1888 in St. Louis, Missouri, the seventh and youngest child of Henry Ware Eliot and Charlotte Stearns. A distinguished family of American aristocrats with a Puritan colonial past, the Eliots traced their ancestry in America to Andrew Eliot, who emigrated from England to Massachusetts in 1670. Eliot's more recent ancestors were leaders in the Unitarian Church, in business, and in education, including a President of Harvard University. Eliot's grandfather, William Greenleaf Eliot, moved to Missouri as a Unitarian missionary and founded the educational institution that would later become Washington University.

After education at Smith Academy in St. Louis and Milton Academy in Massachusetts, Eliot attended Harvard University as an undergraduate from 1906 to 1909. Among professors who influenced him were the New Humanist critic Irving Babbitt and the poet and philosopher George Santayana. Eliot became interested in modern French literature, and was influenced by the work of Baudelaire, Mallarmé, Jules Laforgue, and other French Symbolists, writing poems in imitation of them and in various other styles. He was on the editorial board of the *Harvard Advocate*, to which he contributed seven poems.

After receiving his bachelor's degree, Eliot continued his studies at Harvard as a graduate student in philosophy, also studying Indic philology and Sanskrit. In 1911 he traveled to Europe and attended the lectures of French philosopher Henri Bergson (1859–1941) at the Sorbonne, and after two more years of graduate work at Harvard, took a travelling fellowship to Germany and Merton College, Oxford, where he completed a dissertation on British idealist philosopher F. H. Bradley (1846–1924). World War I prevented him from returning to Harvard to take his doctoral exams in 1916, and though his dissertation was accepted, he never completed the doctorate. His delayed stay in Europe proved to be important in determining his ultimate choice of poetry over philosophy and of

England over America as permanent residence. At this time he wrote some of the poems that would become his first book, including "Preludes" and "The Love Song of J. Alfred Prufrock."

In 1914 Eliot met Ezra Pound in London. Pound immediately identified Eliot's poetry as extraordinary and facilitated the publishing of "Prufrock" in Harriet Monroe's Chicago-based literary magazine, *Poetry*, in June 1915. Eliot found himself in the middle of an exciting and innovative period in art and literature, exchanging ideas with Pound and artist and writer Wyndham Lewis (1882–1957) about "Imagism," "Vorticism," and other new poetic theories and practices. His first volume of poems, *Prufrock and Other Observations*, appeared in 1917.

Persuaded by Pound and others to remain in England, his decision was solidified by his impulsive marriage to Vivien Haigh-Wood, a bright and vivacious but mentally unstable woman. Their marriage was by many accounts disastrous, marked by the continual strain of her deteriorating mental and physical health. Though Eliot's family disapproved of the match and his decision not to return to Harvard, the couple settled in London, where Eliot worked as a schoolteacher while pursuing editorial and reviewing work. In 1917 he took a job in foreign finance at Lloyd's Bank of London where he worked for eight years.

While the period between 1915 and 1927 was especially difficult for Eliot in his personal life, his literary career was burgeoning. In 1920 he published *The Sacred Wood*, a collection of essays that put forth his neo-traditionalist views and some of his most famous critical generalizations, especially in "Tradition and the Individual Talent" and "Hamlet," where he introduces the term "objective correlative" to describe a set of objects or a situation that the poet uses to evoke a particular emotion. From this early criticism Eliot takes an anti-Romantic stance, valuing John Donne (1572–1631) and other metaphysical poets higher than the Romantics and privileging "sensuous apprehension of thought," a poetry prior to a "dissociation of sensibility" in which thought and feeling are unified.

The strain of overwork and his wife's health problems led Eliot to suffer from a nervous breakdown of his own in late 1921. He took a leave of absence from Lloyd's Bank and went to Margate on the southeast coast of England for rest, then on to Switzerland for psychiatric treatment. Much of *The Waste Land* was completed at this time, compiled from earlier fragments, shorter poems, and new work that reflects Eliot's personal crisis. The poem was published in 1922 and won the prestigious Dial Award. Regaining his health, Eliot became the founding editor of the influential journal *The Criterion* (1922–1939) and in 1925 joined Faber & Gwyer (later Faber & Faber) publishers, where he worked as its literary director for most of his life. Eliot had already achieved considerable stature as a critic, and from this position of influence was soon considered by many to be the preeminent man of letters in the Anglo-American world.

In 1927, perhaps the most decisive year in his life, Eliot converted to Anglo-Catholicism and was baptized and confirmed in the Church of England. As a High Church Anglican, Eliot adopted religious beliefs that were sympathetic to the liturgical forms and styles of Roman Catholicism and that emphasized mystery and authority, an explicit rejection of the Unitarianism of his New England family. (Unitarianism, broadly speaking, does not accept Christ's divinity and bases its belief system on ethical behavior and optimism about human progress.) Eliot's conversion to orthodox Christianity was accompanied by two other self-defining choices. He assumed British citizenship and defined his political position as conservative and royalist, a stance against democracy and against the leftist radicalism dominant among artists and literary intellectuals at the time. He also defined himself as a classicist in literature, avowing the classical standards of restraint, discipline, and proportion at a time when the dominant sensibilities were a rejuvenated romanticism that privileged self expression and a "spontaneous overflow" of emotion.

The three decades that followed have been called the "Age of Eliot," so influential was his criticism. In addition to literary criticism, he published several volumes of social criticism that put forth his orthodox views. Eliot continued to publish collections of poems and several plays, among which *Murder in the Cathedral* (1935) was his most successful. In 1932, after separating from his wife, he returned to the United States for the first time in 18 years and delivered the Charles Eliot Norton Lectures at Harvard. Thereafter he continued to travel and lecture widely as a distinguished elder statesman of British letters. In 1944 he published *The Four*

Quartets, a moving exploration of belief and time that many consider his masterpiece. He was awarded both the Nobel Prize and the British Order of Merit in 1948.

Ten years after Vivien's death in 1947, Eliot married Valerie Fletcher, a union he described as giving him the only happy period in his life other than childhood. He died on January 4, 1965, at the age of 76. ❀

Thematic Analysis of
"The Love Song of J. Alfred Prufrock"

First published in *Poetry*, the leading magazine of the avant garde, in 1915, "The Love Song of J. Alfred Prufrock" is Eliot's first major poem. By juxtaposing fragments of voices, images, and scenes, Eliot constructs the persona we call "Prufrock," evoking the frustrated inner life of a speaker who seems to be undergoing a mid-life crisis of nervous anxiety. The text suggests that the character of Prufrock is that of a slightly neurotic anti-hero whose indecision and excess of self-consciousness stall him in his efforts to express himself and to approach the woman he desires. Beyond his fear of sexual rejection, Prufrock's inability to communicate implies a deeper conflict—a despair over spiritual inertness. Through this disjointed interior monologue Eliot creates an ironic love song that vividly represents a modern consciousness.

The poem begins with an epigraph from Dante's *Inferno*, Book 27, in which the spirit of Guido da Montefeltro, not realizing that Dante is alive and only visiting hell, agrees to tell his story, believing that Dante cannot return to spread his infamy on earth. From the outset of Eliot's poem, then, we have a sense that we are speaking with the damned, a speaker trapped in some kind of hell. We also perceive a sense of irony, since the message is indeed carried "from the abyss" to our ears.

The opening line, "Let us go then, you and I," invites us to imagine strolling "When the evening is spread out against the sky," but our expectation of romantic reverie is quickly undercut by the macabre image of "a patient etherised upon a table"—the world out cold. Details of observed surroundings are quickly absorbed into the speaker's thought process, the path through the streets leading to the abstract and unnamed "tedious argument" and "overwhelming ques-tion." This conversion of expectation to numb disappointment, and of outwardness to inwardness, persists as the poem takes us deeper into Prufrock's mental landscape.

The scene changes from urban exterior to a room where "women come and go / Talking of Michaelangelo." The rhyme suggests idle tea party chitchat—trivialization of art as the topic of the day. These lines repeat, emphasizing the tedium of the chic but superficial world Prufrock inhabits. After the false cheer of the initial invitation, the third stanza returns to the urban landscape at nightfall, Prufrock jaded by the usual shallow pleasures of the bourgeois social gathering and looking distractedly out the window. In the extended metaphor of the yellow fog as a cat-like creature, Eliot animates the dirty city with an image that is both domestic and disturbing.

The repetition of "And indeed there will be time" suggests boredom, the word *time* recurring eight times in the fourth stanza alone: Prufrock has too much time on his hands. Allusion to Hesiod's *Works and Days* conveys the irony that Prufrock's "works and days of hands" are not heroic acts but "a hundred indecisions." With "a hundred visions and revisions," Prufrock defers any impulse to act and prolongs his anxiety. He is insecure about his thinning hair and his attire, paranoid that he is being mocked. For Prufrock "there will be time," not to experience life, but "to prepare a face," to pose and to equivocate. The line-break after "Do I dare" suspends the reader in mid-question, then drops to the grandiose "Disturb the universe?" Prufrock's impotent flailings cannot propel him forward, let alone affect the cosmos.

By repeating phrases, Eliot emphasizes the circularity of a thought process that gets nowhere. As Prufrock turns his attention to a woman and the problems of communicating with her, he repeats and revises his question: "how should I presume?" He attempts to be confident, his necktie "asserted by a simple pin," but soon finds himself pinned down, "formulated, sprawling on a pin," squirming under a glance and unable to escape the banalities of small talk, "a formulated phrase." Images of body parts throughout the poem suggest that the human figures he sees are likewise formulated, severed from a sense of wholeness or meaningfulness. Prufrock sees only the woman's arms lying on the table, erotically objectified and unattached to human agency or feeling.

Three images interrupt Prufrock's attempt to muster the courage to speak. In the image of "smoke that rises from the pipes," the line-break at first suggests a view of smokestacks in an industrial city, but the next line telescopes in on pipes smoked by lonely men. This image of human isolation in urban grit is followed by a startlingly dehumanizing moment: "I should have been a pair of ragged claws / Scuttling across the floors of silent seas." The self is reduced to dismembered body parts that are not even human, but crustacean, bottom-feeding.

This extreme of anti-sociability is in turn followed by the drowsy malaise of "Asleep . . . tired . . . or it malingers." Prufrock lingers in a lethargic and sickly atmosphere.

Eliot uses rhyme and meter variably throughout the poem, often for wryly comic effect, as in the lines: "Have known the evenings, mornings, afternoons, / I have measured out my life with coffee spoons. . . ." Prufrock's sense of overfamiliarity and ennui is punctuated by the coyness of the end-rhyme. Rhyme has a similar trivializing effect in the lines "Should I, after tea and cakes and ices, / Have the strength to force the moment to its crisis?" Prettified social rituals render Prufrock's concerns ridiculous. As the poem proceeds, this ironic and interrogative mode continues, suggesting that Prufrock wishes to reach some kind of authentic connection, but is unable to stop doubting himself.

Searching for a figure who will represent his predicament, Prufrock morbidly sees himself as a pathetic, balding John the Baptist, his head "brought in upon a platter," referring to the story of Salome, who danced for Herod in exchange for the prophet's head. Prufrock imagines himself as a degraded prophet, not one who announces a great dispensation of love as John the Baptist preceded Christ, but the herald of "no great matter." He announces nothing, in fact, and sees his life as a waste. He fears the "eternal Footman," and imagines Death snickering at him.

The mundane matters of "the cups, the marmalade, the tea" appear again. Too uptight to make a move, Prufrock worries that his effort to communicate might be misconstrued and that his attempt would be aborted by the woman's superficial insouciance. Trying to work up momentum, he wonders how he might have "squeezed the universe into a ball," echoing the image of intense sexual passion in Andrew Marvell's (1621–1678) "To His Coy Mistress." Eliot then invokes another biblical figure for comparison, Lazarus, raised from the dead in the gospel story (John 11:1–44). Prufrock imagines that he also has a dramatic revelation to tell, a tale from the realm of the dead that the poem's epigraph prefigures, but he is prevented from voicing it, paralyzed by fear that he will miss the mark and be rebuffed.

The poem is constructed in cycles of what critic Denis Donoghue calls "a willed and desperate working up of energy followed inevitably by lassitude." In Prufrock's world, the ordinary business of discussing novels and watching skirts trail along the floor makes any energetic attempts at revelation appear ludicrous. Exasperated, Prufrock exclaims "It is impossible to say just what I mean!" The exclamation is followed by a powerful and peculiar image: "as if a magic lantern threw the nerves in patterns on a screen." The exterior visual field becomes a map of Prufrock's interior nervous state, a vivid pattern that displays his tension and distress.

In a delayed answer to the question "Have I the strength to force the moment to its crisis?" Prufrock exclaims, "No! I am not Prince Hamlet, nor was meant to be." By comparing Prufrock to the literary figure with the most famous indecisions, Eliot emphasizes Prufrock's self-deprecation. Prufrock denies himself a major role, insisting that he is merely "an attendant lord," like Polonius, who gives out advice and is "full of high sentence, but a bit obtuse." Prufrock identifies with a Polonius-like "meticulous" and "ridiculous" figure, "Almost, at times, the Fool." This intense self-consciousness leads to the melodramatic "I grow old . . . I grow old," but the lament is deflated by the comic rhyme that follows, "I shall wear the bottoms of my trousers rolled."

The poem concludes with a fantasy of erotic connection. Prufrock wonders if he has the sensual daring to "eat a peach," and longs to walk along a beach where he will hear mermaids sing. Their song is not directed toward him, he admits self-pityingly, but he still envisions a starkly beautiful, other worldly landscape where "the wind blows the water white and black." Eliot ends the poem with a paradoxical image of spiritual death: we do not drown in the "chambers of the sea," in the fantasy of sensuous paradise and sleep, but drown when we are woken to the tedious reality of "human voices."

Eliot's use of Prufrock as an ironic mask allows him to convey a sense of isolation and alienation, the self imprisoned in a horror of boredom and anxiety. As the continued popularity of this poem attests, Eliot's Prufrock gives voice to a familiar sense of insecurity and inner turmoil, vividly evoking the self-conscious involutions of a modern mind. ❀

Critical Views on
"The Love Song of J. Alfred Prufrock"

CONRAD AIKEN ON "PRUFROCK" AS PSYCHOLOGICAL PORTRAIT

[Conrad Aiken (1889–1973), American writer and critic, went to Harvard with Eliot and maintained a friendship with him for most of his life. In this 1919 review, Aiken compares Eliot to other contemporary writers and describes "Prufrock" as a highly introspective form of psychological realism that risks being too idiosyncratic.]

Mr. T. S. Eliot, whose book *Prufrock and Other Observations* is really hardly more than a pamphlet, is also a realist, but of a different sort. Like Mr. Wilfred Wilson Gibson, Mr. Eliot is a psychologist; but his intuitions are keener; his technique subtler. For the two semi-narrative psychological portraits which form the greater and better part of his book, "The Love Song of J. Alfred Prufrock" and "The Portrait of a Lady," one can have little but praise. This is psychological realism, but in highly subjective or introspective vein; whereas Mr. Gibson, for example, gives us, in the third person, the reactions of an individual to a situation which is largely external (an accident, let us say), Mr. Eliot gives us, in the first person, the reactions of an individual to a situation for which to a large extent his own character is responsible. Such work is more purely autobiographic than the other—the field is narrowed, and the terms are idiosyncratic (sometimes almost blindly so). The dangers of such work are obvious: one must be certain that one's mental character and idiom are sufficiently close to the norm to be comprehensible or significant. In this respect, Mr. Eliot is near the borderline. His temperament is peculiar, it is sometimes, as remarked heretofore, almost bafflingly peculiar, but on the whole it is the average hyperaesthetic one with a good deal of introspective curiosity; it will puzzle many, it will delight a few. Mr. Eliot writes pungently and sharply, with an eye for unexpected and vivid details, and, particularly in the two longer poems and in "The Rhapsody of a Windy Night," he shows himself to be an exceptionally acute technician. Such free rhyme as this, with irregular line lengths, is difficult to write well, and Mr. Eliot does it well enough to make one wonder whether such a form is not what the adorers of free verse will eventually have to come to. In the rest of Mr. Eliot's volume one finds the piquant and the trivial in about equal proportions.

—Conrad Aiken, from *Scepticisms: Notes on Contemporary Poetry* (Knopf, 1919), in *T. S. Eliot: A Selected Critique,* ed. Leonard Unger (New York: Russell & Russell, 1966), p. 3.

CHRISTOPHER RICKS ON THE NAME "J. ALFRED PRUFROCK"

[Christopher Ricks is a distinguished scholar of Romantic, Victorian, and Modern poetry and author of several books, including *Milton's Grand Style* (1963), *Keats and Embarrassment* (1974), and *T. S. Eliot and Prejudice* (1988), an important study of Eliot's anti-Semitism, from which this extract about Eliot's most famous title character is taken.]

Then, back in 1917, before ever you entered upon reading a line of poetry by Mr. T. S. Eliot, you would have been met by the title of the first poem in this, his first book of poems: "The Love Song of J. Alfred Prufrock." At once the crystalline air is thick with incitements to prejudice. For we are immediately invited, or incited, to think and to feel our way through a prejudicial sequence. First, as often with prejudice, comes a concession: that of course a man cannot be blamed for being called Prufrock. Second, that nevertheless the name does have comical possibilities, given not only the play of "frock" against "pru"—prudent, prudish, prurient—but also the suggestive contrariety between splitting the name there, at *pru* and *frock*, as against splitting it as *proof* and *rock*. And, third, that therefore a man in these circumstances might be well advised to call himself John A. Prufrock or J. A. Prufrock, rather than to risk the roll, the rise, the carol, the creation of "J. Alfred Prufrock." Maugham is a name that could countenance W. Somerset as its herald; W. Somerset Prufrock would have been another story-teller. And then we are further invited to think and to feel that should Mr. Prufrock, as is his right, plump for J. Alfred Prufrock, he must not then expect the words "The Love Song of" to sit happily in his immediate vicinity.

The tax returns of J. Alfred Prufrock, fine, but a love song does not harmonize with the rotund name, with how he has chosen to think of himself, to sound himself. He has, after all, chosen to issue his name in a form which is not only formal but unspeakable: no one, not even the most pompous self-regarder, could ever introduce himself as, or be addressed as, J. Alfred Prufrock. He has adopted a form for his name which is powerfully appropriate to a certain kind of page but not to the voice, and which is therefore for ever inimical to the thought of love's intimacy. "I'm in love." "Who's the lucky man?" "J. Alfred Prufrock." Inconceivable . . .

Unjust, of course, these incitements. What's in a name? Yet even with something like a name, which is usually given and not chosen, we manage to exercise choices, to adopt a style which becomes our man, or, if we are Prufrock, to wear our name with a difference. Then a name starts to become so mingled with its owner as to call in question which is doing the owning.

"The Love Song of J. Alfred Prufrock:" even while the title tempts us—not necessarily improperly—to suspect things about the man, it raises the question of whether we are entitled to do so. Can we deduce much from so localized a thing as how a man chooses to cast his name? Can we deduce anything? But then can we imagine that one either could or should refrain from doing any deducing? Straws in the wind are often all that we have to go on. "And should I have the right to smile?:" the question ends the succeeding poem, "Portrait of a Lady," but it is a question that haunts the whole book.

As so often with prejudice, one kind of categorizing melts into another. For the teasing speculation as to what sort of man names himself in such a way, especially given "Prufrock" as his climax, merges itself in the class question, not just what class of man but what social class. Calling oneself J. Alfred Prufrock has an air of prerogative and privilege. The class presumption in turn brings a whole culture and society with it.

—Christopher Ricks, *T. S. Eliot and Prejudice* (Berkeley: University of California Press, 1988), 2–4.

DONALD J. CHILDS ON ELIOT'S MEDICAL METAPHORS

[Donald J. Childs, Associate Professor of English at the University of Ottawa, is the author of *T. S. Eliot: Mystic, Son, and Lover* (1997). In this essay, Childs observes that the metaphor of the "patient etherised," and the split of consciousness and unconsciousness it suggests, resonates throughout Eliot's poetry and philosophical writing.]

One of T. S. Eliot's favorite images is that of a patient spread out upon an examination table. The most famous patient appears at the beginning of Eliot's literary career in "The Love Song of J. Alfred Prufrock" (1911): "Let us go then, you and I, / When the evening is spread out against the sky / Like a patient etherised upon a table." The same image appears a decade afterwards in prose when John Middleton Murry (Eliot's regular intellectual sparring partner) is spread out upon the same table: "It is . . . a real pleasure, an exceptional pleasure, to have a patient like Mr. Murry extended on the operating table; we need our sharpest instruments, and steadiest nerves, if we are to do him justice." It also appears near the end of Eliot's poetic career in *East Coker* (1940):

> The wounded surgeon plies the steel
> That questions the distempered part;
> Beneath the bleeding hands we feel
> The sharp compassion of the healer's art. . . .
> (*Poems*, p.181)

The most important occurrence of the image, however, is in Eliot's dissertation, "Experience and the Objects of Knowledge in the Philosophy of F. H. Bradley" (1916), for it is the development of the image in this text that is echoed in its subsequent appearance as metaphor in the poetry and prose.

By 1940, Eliot is presumably responding to the appearance of the same medical metaphor in the work of a younger generation. As W. H. Auden's editor at Faber and Faber in the 1930s, Eliot regularly encountered this metaphorical expression of Auden's desire for a Marxist healer of the sick modern world. Eliot's "wounded surgeon" is both a conservative Christian revision of Auden's usage (a revision Auden was soon to accept) and a reminder to a younger generation that Eliot had been using the metaphor since his "Prufrock" days.

Analysis of the metaphor's appearance over the years, however, reveals that it also regularly marks the point in Eliot's work of crises concerning the relationship between self and society and the relationship between consciousness and unconsciousness—crises first recognized in Prufrock's split between "you and I," next articulated in metaphysical and epistemological terms in Eliot's dissertation, then explained in his literary criticism as a matter of the relationship between tradition and the individual talent, and finally defined in *The Idea of a Christian Society* (1939) and *Notes Toward the Definition of Culture* (1948) in socio-political terms. In the end, the metaphor marks the eruption into various Eliot texts of his recognition in the dissertation that there is no escape from the hermeneutic circle that involves and revolves as physician and patient both self and not-self, on the one hand, and consciousness and unconsciousness, on the other.

—Donald J. Childs, "Etherised Upon a Table: T. S. Eliot's Dissertation and Its Metaphorical Operations," *Journal of Modern Literature* 18 (1993): 381–2.

LEE OSER ON ELIOT AND PURITANISM

[Lee Oser teaches at Millikin University and is the author of several articles on T. S. Eliot. In this extract, Oser describes how Eliot breaks with the traditions of his immediate family and ancestors by repudiating American Puritan iconography.]

From Eliot's perspective the figure of John the Baptist prophesying was very probably a cliché, a tenuous link to Puritan traditions that were becoming part of the dead past. George Santayana, who taught Eliot at Harvard, had enjoyed a sally at the expense of Puritan cultural and literary traditions by having a fictional undergraduate describe Walt Whitman as "the voice of nature crying in the wilderness of convention" (cf. Matt. 3:3). Following Laforgue's example, Eliot outdid his teacher in the sheer force of his iconoclasm: the *Moralités légendaires* had presented the Baptist in an aspect ripe with expressive possibilities for a disaffected late-Puritan writer circa

1910. In "The Love Song of J. Alfred Prufrock" the prophet no longer prophesies in the American wilderness; instead he is silenced and somewhat comically disfigured. With the image of Prufrock's "head . . . brought in upon a platter," Eliot disrupted a long tradition of American Puritan iconography and implicitly repudiated a legacy of mission and prophetic calling that survived within his immediate family.

A second element in the passage, which immediately precedes the reference to John the Baptist, elucidates the depth of Eliot's engagement with American Puritanism. Prufrock's self-portrait of weeping, prayer, and fasting (line 81) recalls the ritual day of humiliation that Puritan New England had formerly observed in response to social disaster. The Fast Day, the last vestige of the day of humiliation, was not formally abolished in Massachusetts until 1894. A book published in Boston in 1895, W. Love's *The Fast and Thanksgiving Days of New England,* underscores Eliot's connection to the Puritan tradition of fasts by citing the Reverend Andrew Eliot's "A Sermon Preached on the Publick Fast." Andrew, a Congregationalist pastor at Boston's New North Church during the revolutionary period, was the poet's great-great-great-grandfather; in 1919 Eliot would request "sermons of Andrew Eliot" in a letter to his mother. Like the allusion to John the Baptist, Prufrock's fasting bespeaks an intimate knowledge of the religious traditions of New England, and implies the breakdown of those traditions.

Much of the poem's skewed sermonizing is directed by the author at his own heritage. Prufrock's parody of the biblical "Preacher" in Ecclesiastes shows Eliot in full revolt against his ancestors. In the following passage, references to time evoke a missing narrative of history and its homiletic expression, an attempt to reclaim a sense of "purpose under heaven" (Eccles. 3:1). Freed from history, wholly subjective, time becomes the medium of a poet without a mission [see lines 23–34]. A mock preacher celebrating a eucharist of "toast and tea," Prufrock lampoons the biblical idiom with sonorous but empty phrases of murder and creation. Eliot is suggesting that the American Puritan errand, the legacy of theocratic preachers, has failed to find present-day continuators: "all the works and days of hands / That lift and drop a question on your plate" implies a momentous inheritance of others' time and labor that, in the trivial setting of genteel society, can no longer inspire a spirit of self-sacrifice. The situation has its devilish side for the poet, who found his epigraph in Dante's *Inferno*. In the persona of Prufrock, Eliot cannot in good conscience accept the solace of aesthetic pleasure: to escape, self-indulgently, into the subjective time of the poem, the vehicle of his wordplay and imagery, is to admit the loss of a redemptive history that it is his duty to realize.

—Lee Oser, "Charlotte Eliot and 'The Love Song of J. Alfred Prufrock,'" *Modern Philology* 94.2 (1996): 198–9.

Thematic Analysis of
"La Figlia Che Piange"

"La Figlia Che Piange" is the last poem in Eliot's first book, *Prufrock and Other Observations* (1917). The title, Italian for "the daughter who weeps," refers to a marble tablet depicting a young girl that Eliot had looked for, but never found, on a trip to Italy. With its gracefulness and lyricism, the poem stands in contrast to the bleaker and more cynical poems in the volume, but its vision is not as straightforwardly beautiful as it first appears. The epigraph, from Virgil's *Aeneid* Book I, asks "Maiden, by what name will I know you?" In the passage from which the epigraph is taken, Aeneas does not recognize his mother, Venus, who appears before him disguised as a young huntress. Eliot's speaker also stands enthralled before the image of a young woman of unknown identity. The poem addresses the difficulty of the attempt to capture such elusive beauty in poetic language, an attempt that continues to be altered by the vicissitudes of memory and desire.

Several critics have proposed that biographical circumstances shed light on the poem's significance. While at Harvard in 1913, Eliot had met and courted Emily Hale, an affair that was apparently platonic. The two had acted together in amateur theatricals, and once while at Oxford, Eliot had sent her flowers to commemorate another performance. Eliot's La Figlia, with her arms full of flowers on stage, suggests that an emotional memory of this early attachment might have inspired the poem.

The poem opens with series of commands that sound like a director instructing an actor or an artist posing a model. The girl is told to "stand on the highest pavement of the stair," an elevated position from which she may be viewed. She is turned by the observer, directed to "lean on a garden urn" so that she might be seen in the best light. She is then told to manipulate light with graceful motion—"weave, weave the sunlight in your hair"—curiously both acting upon the light and acted upon by it, seen even more flatteringly. Similarly, the speaker is both commanding and receptive, controlling her with his gaze, imagining her as he chooses, but also recording an impression that has troubling sensuous power over him.

The instruction "clasp your flowers to you with a pained surprise— / Fling them to the ground and turn / With a fugitive resentment in your eyes" is particularly theatrical, as if La Figlia were the heroine of a melodrama. As Eliot indulges these histrionic gestures of "fugitive resentment," her ephemeral grudge, he also belies some irony. By describing the girl as if *telling her* to put on "pained surprise," and not simply presenting that emotion as interpretable in an image he ostensibly sees, he makes clear that the poetic image itself is inherently staged, an affectation, not an authentic response.

After the dramatic, active verbs of the first stanza (such as "stand," "clasp," and "fling"), the second stanza opens with a compound grammatical construction. The past conditional tense—"So I would have had him leave"—*distances* the observer from the scene, keeping the matter in the past, and making it only a possibility, not an actuality. As Eliot backs off from the immediacy of the first stanza, he presents the other half of the dramatic situation, the lover who made La Figlia weep. By introducing the third person "him," Eliot triangulates a relation that had previously been only the gazer and the woman gazed upon, the speaker and the "you." Not only is there now a "he" to contend with, but a "we" and an "I." The pronouns confuse the matter of who desires whom, keeping the poem's speaker at a safer distance.

The speaker scripts the scene as he "would have had" it, the woman left behind and grieving over her lost lover. The image is transformed through an act of will that places it in the realm of abstract and philosophical terms—soul, mind, and body. Eliot presents two analogies for the desertion: "he" leaves "her," "As the soul leaves the body torn and bruised," and "As the mind deserts the body it has used." The analogies align "soul" and "mind" with the man and "body" with the woman, traditionally gendered terms, and in doing so the comparison suggests an undertone of sexual violence. Eliot toys with the potential for figurative language to blur the terms of the initial comparison and resonate other dramatic possibilities, even cruel ones. Though it is rendered abstractly, the memory of the image continues to exert its force.

The speaker wishes for "some way incomparably light and deft" to mediate this force, "some way we both should understand," that is contained within the easy proprieties of "a smile and a shake of a hand." But the effort to control the image, to pose it, leads to uneasiness. "La Figlia," he admits, "compelled my imagination" with a lyrical intensity that persisted "many days, / Many days and many hours. . . ." Even an image carefully constructed as after-the-fact sparks a present tense wonderment: "I wonder how they should have been together!" Because of the earlier slippage of pronouns, "they" is easily read as "we," as if the speaker himself was implicated in the passion—not merely a distant observer of a static object. "She turned away" suggests a personal and poignant loss.

The poem is remarkable for its musicality and use of leit motifs. Unlike poems that seem to have been inspired by an idea of writing "a poem about X," this poem suggests that Eliot started writing it with simply a rhythm in his head. The incantatory power of lines like "her hair over her arms and her arms full of flowers" derives from its cadence: the sound seems to gather momentum ahead of the sense, with the rhythm suggesting a tumbling of hair and flowers, not vice versa. Perfectly chimed end-rhymes give satisfaction in their own right, and sonic possibilities within one line tend to invite a rhyming word in the next, as "weave" invites "leave" and then "grieve." The repeated "so" sounds of the second stanza perhaps suggested the word "soul" for its acoustic affinity first, then for its suggestion of semantic meaning. The poem's phrasings are carefully modulated and complex. Throughout, Eliot works both with and against iambics, fluctuating between lyric undulations and a harder prose feel.

The last three lines of the poem suggest a commentary on the poet's own process. The speaker ends self-consciously, cryptically remarking, "I should have lost a gesture and a pose." As Peter Ackroyd points out, "the incantation itself is so evidently concocted that it deliberately invites skepticism about its nature. When the poet seems most himself, he is an actor watching his own performance."[1] By the end of the poem, the poet/speaker has been staged as La Figlia has been staged. Eliot's own "weaving" has revealed the obliquities and ambiguities implied in poetic stagings of desire. With the word "cogitations," Eliot attempts to intellectualize the persistent influence of the girl's image, to render the poem an example of what he praised in the Metaphysical poets, a "sensuous apprehension of thought." But passion infused in language continues to trouble him: transformed in memory, the "cogitations" of poetic language "still amaze / The troubled midnight and the noon's repose." ❀

---

[1] Peter Ackroyd, *T. S. Eliot: A Life* (New York: Simon and Schuster, 1984), 80.

Critical Views on
"La Figlia Che Piange"

F. O. MATTHIESSEN ON ELIOT AND HENRY JAMES

[F. O. Matthiessen (1902–1950) was an important critic of American literature. His books include *American Renaissance* (1941), *Henry James: The Major Phase* (1944), and *The Achievement of T. S. Eliot* (1947), from which this extract is taken. Matthiessen compares Eliot's use of pictorial and dramatic impressions to reveal character to similar effects in the work of the novelist Henry James (1843–1916).]

In defining Eliot's particular dramatic quality it is relevant to quote Rémy de Gourmont's brief characterization of symbolism, in his *Book of Masks:* "a tendency to take only the characteristic detail out of life, to pay attention only to the act by which a man distinguishes himself from another man, and to desire only to realize essentials, results." There could hardly be a better account of the way in which Eliot endeavours to portray "human action and human attitudes." He sets out to make his characters actual by confining his description of them to a perceived significant detail or characteristic gesture. This is the method by which he lets us conceive the nature of Princess Volupine [in Eliot's poem "Burbank with a Baedeker, Bleistein with a Cigar"] by means of a glimpse of her outstretched "meagre, blue-nailed, phthisic hand." Or again, he creates the dramatic relevance of the figures who throng Gerontion's [in Eliot's poem, "Gerontion"] memory by the way he shows each of them in action. He wants to intermingle description and event in the manner in which they actually associate in a person's impressions; this is the intention emphasized by his statement that he was stimulated by Henry James' example in *The Aspern Papers* to try "to make a place real not descriptively but by something happening there." What "happens" in Eliot's shorter poems is frequently no more than a single observed impression: a girl standing at the top of a stairway "with a fugitive resentment" in her eyes; a young man handing his cousin the evening paper. Yet, as also in James, there is something both pictorial and dramatic in this single impression, something acutely revelatory of the people described. As James remarked in "The Art of Fiction:"

> What is a picture or a novel that is *not* of character? What else do we
> seek in it and find in it? It is an incident for a woman to stand up
> with her hand resting on a table and look out at you in a certain way;
> or if it be not an incident, I think it will be hard to say what it is. At
> the same time, it is an expression of character.

These sentences might describe the effect of Eliot's "La Figlia che
Piange" equally as well as that of one of James's own stories. The
more one thinks of Eliot in relation to James, the more one realizes
the extent of the similarities between them. They are similarities of
content as well as of method. Both James and Eliot, no less than
Hawthorne, are mainly concerned with what lies behind action and
beneath appearance. In their effort to find the exact situation that
will evoke an impression of the inner life, they are occupied too in
expressing like states of mind and feeling. Prufrock's rankling
inability to give himself to life and the kind of frustration embodied
in Eliot's "Portrait of a Lady" find their parallels many times in
James. But even more significant is the realization that the qualities
of spirit that rise above frustration in Eliot's later poems, as well as
in James's *Portrait of a Lady* or *The Wings of the Dove*, are those
which affirm the value of renunciation, sympathy, and tenderness.
These qualities have long been dominant in the American strain. All
three are to be found in Emily Dickinson, if with a somewhat different effect than in Hawthorne; and the two last are Whitman's
most enduring tones in "When lilacs last in the dooryard bloomed."

—F. O. Matthiessen, *The Achievement of T.S. Eliot* (New York: Oxford
University Press, 1947), 69–70.

GEORGE WILLIAMSON ON ELIOT'S MIXTURE OF MOODS

[George Williamson (1898–1968) was Professor of English
at the University of Chicago and is the author of *The Proper
Wit of Poetry* (1962) and *Seventeenth Century Contexts*
(1969), among other books. In this extract, Williamson
describes Eliot's blending of beauty and cynicism, a technique borrowed from the French poet Jules Laforgue.]

The mixture of moods in "La Figlia Che Piange" (1916) is subtly and effectively integrated. In this vision of the weeping girl the cynical mood cannot expel the former emotion or dispel the aura of the experience. The Virgilian epigraph (*Aeneid* I, 327) recalls the encounter of Venus and Aeneas. Venus, disguised as a maiden asking "have you seen a sister of mine?" is addressed by Aeneas: "O maiden, how may I name thee?" This epitomizes the poem's problem of emotional recollection. In the first section we have the recreation of a vision involving beauty and pain, now beginning to be colored by cynicism—marked, for example, by "fugitive." His later, cynical, mood emerges clearly in the second section, as he defines the emotional values of the parting. As he remembers it now, it resembled the separation of body and soul in a figure which reserves grief for her and release for him, which translates pain into callousness. Then disillusion finds the "way incomparably light and deft," which unites them both in cynical understanding.

The last section records the bare reality in "she turned away," for she did not behave as first described, with romantic exaggeration. Yet he was, and still is, troubled. Though his later mood asserts itself in the reckoning of his loss, he is still troubled by the vision, its beauty and pain remain with him. Now he would mock or deny any emotional concern, but his efforts are vain. This vision of beauty involving pain that is subsequently qualified by disillusion reappears in the imagery which symbolizes mingled longing and frustration in his later poems. For the poet this becomes a central experience and symbol, like the symbolizing of woman which he finds in Dante and Baudelaire. It is imperative to mark the parallel. While it would be perilous to equate them, no clue to his symbols and their meaning is more important. "O maiden, how may I recall thee?" thus acquires an importance beyond this poem, posing a question of emotional harmony.

All of the more significant poems in this volume are Laforgian in their esoteric imagery, their mixture of mood and language, their ironic deployment. I have ignored the lines that are actually lifted from Laforgue, for that sort of borrowing has not the importance to understanding Eliot that is commonly given it. It becomes important, and Laforgian, only when it plays ironically over the surface of other poetry. Otherwise such borrowings can only be considered as integral parts of Eliot's poems, deriving their meaning from them.

To interpret such borrowings by their original context is the surest way to discover that Eliot does not write pastiches. The influence of Laforgue, as Eliot remarks about influence in Pound, is apparent "more as an emotional attitude than in the technique of versification." At least this influence is not less positive in the ironic attitude which translates defections from the ideal into ironic sentiment than in the colloquial and symbolic technique of the verse.

—George Williamson, *A Reader's Guide to T. S. Eliot* (New York: Farrar, Straus & Giroux, 1966), 84–6.

DAVID WARD ON MEMORY

[David Ward (b. 1932) has written several articles on American and South African literature. Here, Ward shows that Eliot's elaborations and revisions of the image of the girl imply the changing constructs of memory, experience, and desire.]

[In Eliot's early poetry] the dissolution of the normal rules of relation, the abandonment of the normal method and sequence of thought is perhaps only so that the poet can allow himself free rein for a modish sequence of "imagistic" verses. But it foreshadows a more complex kind of investigation which begins from the same point.

A fine early example of this more subtle exploration of memory and experience is "La Figlia che Piange," a poem which has suffered from being prematurely popular, and popular for the wrong reasons. It is the poem most likely to appeal to a sensibility not yet attuned to Eliot's frequently bizarre language and his characteristically abrupt changes of tone and mood, but for all that it is a very interesting poem indeed. One might be tempted to speak of it in somewhat the same terms as Eliot speaks of Marvell—"a tough reasonableness beneath the slight lyric grace"—to characterize the delicate, almost fragile phrasing and the lyrical control of movement; but tough and reasonable are neither of them words which would apply: the theme is the uncertain paradoxes of memory and experience, the tone tentative and halting, the contrasts in tonality muted and masked; there is none of the direct assuredness of Marvell—that would be something quite foreign to Eliot's poetic personality.

The poem begins with a memory, as it were arrested in a captured image: a pose, a gesture, a movement and an effect of light; all as perfectly grouped as one could wish a memory to be. But there is some doubt about the realness of the memory. It is a memory in some sense formed by desire and will, or by a sense of aesthetic fitness [lines 8–9] and the memory is still open to augmentation and change; the imagination still compelled to elaborate the parting into something even more delicate and fitting [lines 13–16].

Our memories have curative and aesthetic skills; they will constantly tidy up the past to enable us to live with it, so the past is made through memory a part of the present. And yet another image lies beside the neat but still changing shape remembered—merely as an unformed possibility to trouble and delight the mind, as the "infinitely gentle, infinitely suffering thing" troubles and delights the imagination of the "Preludes" [lines 21–22].

The memory prefers the rôle of *voyeur* to that of friend or lover, and indeed cannot do much else; however unreal the remembered image is, the alternative is a totally different reality world. And like any *voyeur* it prefers fantasy to reality: the gesture, the pose, the movement, the effect of light are "what I would have," a construct of desire. And the construct of desire is further described and developed by a set of metaphors which take the incident still further away from an actual past into a world of ideas [lines 10–12].

Perhaps, on the other hand, we might say that the image of memory itself, hedged around and qualified by its verbal moods, is more abstract and unreal than the metaphors of soul and body which have at least some directness, even some brutality. The image elaborates itself in memory to describe an experience which is lost in the changes of memory, though one thing remains constant; the experience of loss and change within memory, its poignancy made very beautiful by the romantic elaborations of memory. As any actual past recedes, the objective of remembering becomes the memory itself; in this case the memory of something incomplete, unfinished, yet incomparably beautiful. The poem has something in common with the episodes of the hyacinth girl and the rose garden, in which similar incidents of memory are orchestrated into a more complex pattern of memory and desire, and their organization into a larger whole makes these episodes far more resonant with unstated or half-stated meaning. But, within its limits, "La Figlia che Piange" is a nearly perfect little poem.

—David Ward, *T. S. Eliot Between Two Worlds: A Reading of T. S. Eliot's Poetry and Plays* (Boston: Routledge & Kegan Paul, 1973), 25–7.

RONALD BUSH ON THE DANDY AND EMOTIONAL DETACHMENT

[Ronald Bush is the author of *The Genesis of Pound's Cantos* (1976), *T. S. Eliot, the Modernist in History* (1991), and *Prehistories of the Future: The Primitivist Project and the Culture of Modernism* (1995). In this extract, Bush examines the poem as evidence of a "Prufrock-like" psychic struggle.]

Prufrock's love song moves toward an erotic vision of a group of women at a tea party. Their arms, "braceleted and white and bare," provoke the insurgence of his buried life, and their pillowed heads push the conflict of his divided selves to the point of crisis. The same moment occurs much amplified in one of Eliot's other early love songs. In "La Figlia Che Piange," the poem Eliot chose to conclude the *Prufrock* volume, the women at the top of the stairs are telescoped into one woman, who dominates the poem and who focuses the ambivalence of Eliot's speaker toward his emotional life. . . .

. Faced with the image of the girl in his revery, the dandified speaker of this poem responds with a Prufrock-like doubleness. Threatened by his desires, he retreats into the weary irony of a self-consciously arch phrase [lines 5–6].

But the needs of his emotional life refuse to be denied. In the midst of his ironic detachment, we sense the power of an obsession. The poetic organization of the first stanza stresses what would in any case be four emphatic monosyllables [lines 1–4].

The force behind these imperatives, all of which attempt to freeze an action into one definable gesture, suggests just how much psychic energy Eliot's speaker must exert to keep the girl's image from becoming vivid and uncomfortable. These stage directions are more than the reflections of an achieved aesthetic detachment. They are part of the poem's inner psychic struggle, in which the dandy anxiously battles to immobilize the girl's image in a tableau fixed and colored by the conventions of his acquired self. Try as he may, though, his attempts prove ineffective. The dandy cannot keep his desire from endowing the girl with a charm as powerful as her ability to unsettle him. And so, in the last line of the first stanza, which is also the end of the poem's first movement, an insurgent burst of lyricism disencumbers the girl's image, and all but effaces the dandy's emotional detachment [line 7].

Then, as so often in Eliot's poetry, the beginning of a new stanza signals a new stage of emotional conflict. In stanza two, the impulses behind the poem's ironic voice regroup and the voice employs stronger measures to avoid involvement. For one thing, the imagined encounter is recast from the imperative to the less immediate conditional perfect form that Eliot also uses near the end of "Prufrock" [lines 8–9].

More obviously, the speaker protects his ironic stance by splitting himself up into a participant lover ("he") and "I," the detached observer who is now entirely outside the encounter. But even these stratagems cannot ward off the suppressed emotion that is the poem's most distinctive signature. This time, two similes follow the re-enacted scene, and they betray an increased intensity that clarifies the emotional significance of the young girl [lines 10–13].

The dandy, by comparing the lover's desertion of his beloved to the mind's desertion of an exploited body, suggests that at some level, man and girl, lover and beloved, are projections of his own psyche, and that *la figlia*, the young girl, is an image of his own emotional life. It is not surprising, then, that the similes are sympathetically weighted toward the body. Though the word order connects the speaker with mind and soul—the agents of a New England sensibility—the dandy's strongest identification is with the buried emotional life suggested by the heart, the body and the girl. The twice-deserted corpse in his similes thus presents the suppressed desolation characteristic of his own history. He has been cut off from his vital center by an acquired self, and the split seems like the separation of death. Like Prufrock, he is suspended between two identities, unable to enjoy either. It is this tension, this torment, that is mirrored in the syntax of the first simile, where either the body or the soul can be modified by "torn and bruised."

—Ronald Bush, *T. S. Eliot: A Study in Character and Style* (New York: Oxford University Press, 1983), 11–13.

TONY PINKNEY ON ELIOT'S DEPICTION OF WOMEN

[Tony Pinkney is the author of *D. H. Lawrence and Modernism* (1990) and *Women in the Poetry of T. S. Eliot: A Psychoanalytical Approach* (1984). Taking a psychoanalytic approach, Pinkney analyzes the poem's expression of an exploitative and destructive impulse toward women.]

If woman in Eliot is in one aspect all that resists language, if she is nameless because she threatens a psychotic collapse that will reduce language to the non-signifying babble of apes and parrots, then the poetry itself will be the process of resisting that resistance, of conferring a name. Eliot's poems are accordingly not passive "expressions" or "reflections" of psychoanalytic phantasies, but rather *strategies* whereby the adult ego struggles to establish an effective distance over against the psychic conflicts that buffet it. Something of that dialectical relationship between phantasy and ego, reflection and strategy, is given in the very structure of the verbs which govern the opening lines of "La Figlia.". . . Ambivalently situated between imperative and indicative, these verbs at once neutrally report and actively dispose the gestures in question. This ambiguity is in its turn reproduced in what is a central line in a Kleinian interpretation of this poem: the girl's lover would have left "as the soul leaves the body torn and bruised" ". . . . leaves" hovers undecidably between a straightforward sense of "departure"—the soul leaves the torn and bruised body— and a much more sinister implication of agency: the soul *renders* the body torn and bruised. In both cases the brutality of the epithets here is a striking dissonance; they refuse the merely illustrative role the simile would grant them and insist on the felt presence here of a significant phantasy. For "La Figlia," like so many poems in this volume, is governed by the Raskolnikovian staircase and is in quest of "Some way incomparably light and deft" whereby its destructive impulse towards the woman can be at once gratified and evaded.

This end is achieved by the textual splitting that makes the poet simultaneously contemplative observer and dangerous participant in the dramatised situation, a split at the level of structure that gathers up and governs the local ambiguities I noted above. This splitting of the ego is the obverse of a single-minded idealisation of the woman. In so far as an aggressive sexuality does enter the poem it takes the form not of the familiar phallic woman, but of the muted sexual exploitativeness of the poet-lover deserting "the body [he] has used." . . .The repose of noon is thus rather more troubled than "La Figlia" would care to admit, shadowed as it always is by the psychic destructiveness that is its dark underside or subtext. This poem is more successful than most in repressing that subtext, to the point where it has been read as a celebration of "love in the lyrical sense, with no irony in the tone or context." If Eliot's texts are all strategies concerned both to do girls in and to deny the doing, then this comment by F. R. Leavis reveals that strategic sense successfully deployed on a wider scale to effect a denial of violence over the volume as a whole. Yet at the centre of "La Figlia," as of *Prufrock and Other Observations*, stands the stark reminder of all that Eliot's lyricism would deny: "the body torn and bruised."

—Tony Pinkney, *Women in the Poetry of T. S. Eliot: A Psychoanalytic Approach* (London: Macmillan, 1984), 55–7.

Thematic Analysis of
"The Waste Land"

With its complex imagery, multiple voices, and myriad allusions, *The Waste Land* invites seemingly infinite annotation and commentary. The most famous and influential text of literary Modernism, the poem assembles, in its own terms, "a heap of broken images." The effect and significance of this assemblage have been interpreted in various ways, but the poem itself offers the best starting point: one speaker asserts, "These fragments I have shored against my ruins," suggesting that grappling with disparate elements has been a difficult means of sustaining, or attempting to sustain, something vital that threatens to be lost or destroyed.

Through many literary references, especially to Dante, Shakespeare, the Bible, and Restoration drama, Eliot appropriates a historical tradition with a view toward reformulating the materials in a contemporary way. In doing so, he addresses the discontinuity of the Western literary tradition in the modern era, but also transforms and strengthens textual remnants that memorialize it. The footnotes Eliot added to the poem indicate that Jessie Weston's *From Ritual to Romance* inspired much of its symbolism. Some critics have dismissed these notes (as Eliot himself later did) as a spoof on hypererudition, yet aspects of the Holy Grail legend and ancient vegetation myths that Weston discusses are useful guiding lenses through which to read the poem. *The Waste Land* can be read as modern Europe mythologized or allegorized, a dead land struck by spiritual famine and drought, where the Fisher King awaits a period of renewed fertility. The incorporation of other cultural elements throughout the poem, including Greek and Hindu mythologies, offers other perspectives on this sense of intense longing for redemption.

Published in 1922, the poem reflects Eliot's personal crisis at the time as well as larger historical and social concerns. Many early readers considered the poem, with its cultural pessimism, to be a testament to the disillusionment of a generation, an exposition on the manifest despair and spiritual bankruptcy of the years after World War I. In this view, the fragments that make up the poem reflect the fragmented nature of twentieth-century urban life. With possibilities for global transit and communication, as well as global war, developing with alarming velocity, the modern world relies on the rapid transmission of energies, energies that the poem's leaps—its seemingly arbitrary transitions—mimic and imply.

The epigraph, from the *Satyricon* of Petronius (d. AD 66), describes the Cumaean Sibyl, a legendary prophetess who was granted immortality but not immortal youth. By introducing the poem with the Sibyl's wish to die rather than age for eternity, Eliot sets a tone of desperation and suggests a prospect of inevitable and prolonged suffering. In the dedication, echoing Dante's praise of Arnaut Daniel, Eliot credits Ezra Pound with being "the better craftsman." Pound had edited the manuscript of *The Waste Land* and suggested that Eliot cut its nearly 800 lines down to the 434 lines of its published form.

Part I, "The Burial of the Dead," begins with a quasi-prophetic voice sullenly confronting the spring thaw, an opening that recalls Chaucer's General Prologue to *The Canterbury Tales*. The mention of "lilacs," as well as several other important details in the poem, echoes Walt Whitman's elegy for Lincoln, "When Lilacs Last in the Dooryard Bloomed," and reveals an important emotional subtext. In the way that Whitman's poem becomes an elegy for his poetic self, more so than for its ostensible subject, Eliot's poem likewise belies anxiety about the possible loss of his poetic strength.

After this invocation, the persona of Marie, a Lithuanian-German aristocrat, describes a childhood experience of sledding as an important moment of exhilaration and release. Her self-indulgent narrative is juxtaposed with a description of a barren landscape, biblical in its tone and reference—the poem's first waste land. Eliot then interposes part of a song from Wagner's *Tristan und Isolde* in which a sailor longs for his beloved, a sense of being lost at sea that is emphasized in the last line of the verse-paragraph, which translates "empty and waste the sea." This passage also presents the hyacinth girl, who is remembered by a speaker who was unable to respond to her sensuality. His remark, "I was neither / Living nor dead," applies to the emotionally deadened speakers throughout this section.

In the next verse-paragraph, Madame Sosostris practices a debased form of religion by fortune-telling with Tarot cards, ministering comically to the superficial spirituality of people like Mrs. Equitone. The figures of the Hanged Man and the drowned Phoenician Sailor (whose description echoes Shakespeare's *The Tempest* and who will come up again) are foreboding. Modern city dwellers are spiritually lost, lacking proper values, and even damned, as Eliot suggests with the description of the flow of commuters over London Bridge. The line "I had not thought death had undone so many" likens the crowd to the flow of souls into hell in Dante's *Inferno.* In a gesture that condenses space and time, one speaker stops and recognizes a modern man named Stetson, as being from Mylae, a site of the Carthaginian war in 260 BC. Modern London is an "Unreal City," and this highly allusive passage suggests the depth of its infernal corruption. The section ends with the macabre image of a corpse planted in a garden, dug up by a dog. In this world, death is followed only by grotesque exhumation, not resurrection. The last line of the section, a quote from Charles Baudelaire's preface to *Les Fleurs du Mal,* addresses the reader as complicit in the ennui that Eliot condemns.

Part II, "A Game of Chess," opens with a description of a rich woman in a suffocatingly elegant atmosphere that recalls Shakespeare's description of Cleopatra's barge in *Antony and Cleopatra* and Virgil's description of Dido's palace in the *Aeneid.* References to these stories—grand passions that end in suicides—make this woman appear a lifeless sinner by contrast. A painting in the room displays a scene from the myth of Procne and Philomela, a story that Eliot will refer to again. In Ovid's account, King Tereus rapes Philomela, his wife Procne's sister, and cuts out her tongue. She manages to communicate her story to her sister by weaving the scene into a tapestry, and together they avenge themselves on Tereus by killing his son, Itys, and serving him to his father for dinner. Procne and Philomela are turned into a swallow and a nightingale as the enraged king pursues them. With the allusion to this story, an undertone of sexual brutality troubles the lethargy and luxury of this drawing room scene.

Two vivid scenes further Eliot's critique of cultural decadence and spiritual dissatisfaction in the modern world. The first portrays an estranged marriage in which the wife's shrill speech and the husband's morbid mental responses point out the meaninglessness and boredom of their lives. The wife's frantic questioning conveys nervous anxiety and sexual frustration, and the husband's recollection of the image of the drowned man from Ariel's song in *The Tempest* emphasizes their failure to transform the dreadful stasis. The game of chess is a figure for a meaningless sexual act, a way of killing insomniac time. The scene shifts to a pub, where working-class women discuss another married couple, Lil and Albert, whose wretched circumstances have reduced human relationships to matters of lust, bad teeth, abortion, alcohol, and adultery. Throughout the passage, the bartender's insistent last call, "hurry up please it's time," resounds as a warning that death approaches. The section concludes with lines from *Hamlet*, the song of the sexually deranged Ophelia.

Part III, "The Fire Sermon," continues the themes of sexual degeneration and immorality as well as intensifies the poem's mythic elements. The title refers to the Buddha's sermon charging disciples to divest themselves of the consuming fires of human passions. Allusions to Spenser's *Prothalamion*, a wedding song posed in ironic contrast, and Psalm 137, a lament of exiles, emphasize the desolation of the late-autumn scene where the Fisher King waits by the Thames riverbank (or, in another interpretation, where the poet waits.) The repetition of "But at my back . . . I hear," an echo of Andrew Marvell's "To His Coy Mistress," also poses an ironic counterpoint. The Fisher King (or poet-observer) does not hear, as Marvell does, "Time's winged chariot" behind him; instead, he hears the din of an industrial city. In this section, the ironic juxtaposition of heroic quest and sordid contemporary detail, such as vulgar ballads about Mrs. Porter's, a well-known Cairo whorehouse, evokes a bleak spiritual condition.

Eliot then presents two further examples of sexual interactions he depicts as immoral and degenerate. In the first, Mr. Eugenides propositions the speaker with an invitation to a weekend homosexual liaison. In the second, a working woman, a typist, receives the repulsive "young man carbuncular" in her squalid flat, listlessly permitting him to have sex with her. This scene is told through the eyes and voice of the mythical character Tiresias, whom Eliot called "the most important personage in the poem, uniting all the rest." According to Ovid, Tiresias was transformed into a woman when he struck a pair of copulating snakes. Seeing and striking them again seven years later, he was turned back into a man. Since he had experienced sex as both a man and a woman, he was asked to settle a dispute between Jove and Juno over who enjoyed sex more. Tiresias sided with Zeus, who claimed women had more pleasure. Juno, enraged, blinded Tiresias, but Zeus compensated him with the gift of prophesy. Though the seriousness of Eliot's claim that Tiresias is the poem's central figure has been disputed, Tiresias's role as all-seeing spectator, witnessing acts of mechanical and degraded sex, aptly expresses a sense of grief about dehumanized interactions.

Eliot presents another image of London's East End, the busy financial and business district, and then concludes the section with the Song of the Three Thames Daughters. The first stanza presents a word painting of ecological pollution that implies moral pollution, ending with lines that repeat Wagner's refrain of the Rhine-maidens in *Götterdämmerung*. The second stanza's portrayal of Queen Elizabeth I suggests that even in the glorious age of the Virgin Queen sexuality was used for political gain. The three daughters then tell how they lost their virginity, more tawdry scenes of young women undone. They shrug off their downfall, resorting to nihilistic indifference, a feeling one expresses as "I can connect / Nothing with nothing." "The Fire Sermon" ends by likening this collection of sexual anecdotes to an arrival at Carthage, the "cauldron of unholy loves" in Augustine's *Confessions*. With the incantatory repetition of the word *burning*, Eliot draws attention to fire as a symbol of carnal desire and as the medium of purification that will purge it.

Part IV, "Death by Water," presents a full view of Phlebas the Phoenician, the drowned sailor that Madame Sosostris had mentioned and that images from *The Tempest* foreshadowed. Incorporating material from an earlier poem written in French, "Dans le Restaurant," Eliot uses this passage to point out the futility of worldly concerns: profit and loss are rendered meaningless at the bottom of the sea. Phlebas returns to a primitive state, "entering the whirlpool" where death may give rise to new life. The section ends with a universalized warning, a prophesy of impending spiritual and physical death.

Part V, "What the Thunder Said," is a culmination of the poem's multi-voiced and complexly layered systems of reference. Imagery in this section is surreal and hallucinatory, and polyglot quotations are even more quickly compounded, especially in the final verse-paragraph. The lament in the first stanza recalls Christ's agony in the garden at Gethsemane. The poem then moves into an elemental description of a dessicated landscape, a world so parched that it is characterized by a "Dead mountain mouth of carious teeth that cannot spit." In dire thirst, the speaker longs for water and for the revitalizing "water-dripping song" of the hermit-thrush. This song and the reference to the New Testament account of Jesus on the road to Emmaus echo Whitman's *Lilacs* elegy, and through them Eliot suggests the futility of longing for rejuvenation in a landscape where the divine cannot be recognized. If we consider the Grail Legend as the implicit structure of the poem, the scene can also be interpreted as the Knight Quest's approach to the Temple Perilous, a desperate struggle to overcome despair and reach salvation. The struggle takes the quester through the ruins of Western civilization: the cities Eliot lists are the major originary centers of Western culture, with the exclusion of Rome, and they are all, Eliot suggests, subject to decay.

The images that follow—from "bats with baby faces" to "tumbled graves"—have a bizarre and gothic quality. A storm brews; the knight approaches the chapel; the thunder "speaks" over the Ganges. In this passage, Eliot uses the Sanskrit words *datta, dayadhvam, damyata* (give, sympathize, control), from a fable in one of the Hindu Upanishads, to sound a (rather nebulous) moral injunction. Between the thunderclaps, he addresses three views of the self. First, he regrets the self-surrender of passion's "awful daring." Next, the self is imagined as suffering in confinement, like Ugolino in Dante's *Inferno*: hearing the key turn in the lock of the Hunger Tower, Ugolino is left to starve with his sons. Third, the speaker navigates on the sea in a hopeful frenzy, imagining its responsiveness and his own control. Nonetheless, as the poem's leaps suggest, this control is delusional—memory and desire are irremediably fractured, and even the self is fragmented.

In the last movement of the poem, the Fisher King and the poet-speaker are left waiting, hoping rain will fall to relieve the suffering land and renew fertility. A final quick succession of quotes summarizes *The Waste Land*'s obsessive themes: Eliot juxtaposes a nursery rhyme vision of chaos, a line of Dante's about purifying flame, Philomela's wish to become a bird, a statement of nobility in exile, and a moment of madness. The last line of the poem repeats the Sanskrit word *shantih*, "the peace that passes understanding," ending the poem as if it too has evolved toward the status of sacred text. The shored fragments have amounted to the possibility of redemption, though not redemption itself. ❋

Critical Views on
"The Waste Land"

T. S. ELIOT ON "TRADITION AND THE INDIVIDUAL TALENT"

[In this extract from one of his most famous essays, Eliot addresses the poet's relation to the past literary tradition. He rejects the romantic view that poetry should be an out-pouring of emotion and an expression of individual personality: "Poetry is not a turning loose of emotion, but an escape from emotion; it is not an expression of personality, but an escape from personality" (43). *The Waste Land* can be read as one outcome of a poetic process in which the poet's mind acts as a "catalyst" on a large body of cultural and literary materials.]

I am alive to a usual objection to what is clearly part of my pro-gramme for the *métier* of poetry. The objection is that the doctrine requires a ridiculous amount of erudition (pedantry), a claim which can be rejected by appeal to the lives of poets in any pantheon. It will even be affirmed that much learning deadens or perverts poetic sen-sibility. While, however, we persist in believing that a poet ought to know as much as will not encroach upon his necessary receptivity and necessary laziness, it is not desirable to confine knowledge to whatever can be put into a useful shape for examinations, drawing-rooms, or the still more pretentious modes of publicity. Some can absorb knowledge, the more tardy must sweat for it. Shakespeare acquired more essential history from Plutarch than most men could from the whole British Museum. What is to be insisted upon is that the poet must develop or procure the consciousness of the past and that he should continue to develop this consciousness throughout his career.

What happens is a continual surrender of himself as he is at the moment to something which is more valuable. The progress of an artist is a continual self-sacrifice, a continual extinction of personality.

There remains to define this process of depersonalization and its relation to the sense of tradition. It is in this depersonalization that art may be said to approach the condition of science. I therefore invite you to consider, as a suggestive analogy, the action which takes place when a bit of finely filiated platinum is introduced into a chamber containing oxygen and sulphur dioxide.

Honest criticism and sensitive appreciation is directed not upon the poet but upon the poetry. If we attend to the confused cries of the newspaper critics and the susurrus of popular repetition that follows, we shall hear the names of poets in great numbers; if we seek not Blue-book knowledge but the enjoyment of poetry, and ask for a poem, we shall seldom find it. I have tried to point out the importance of the relation of the poem to other poems by other authors, and suggested the conception of poetry as a living whole of all the poetry that has ever been written. The other aspect of this Impersonal theory of poetry is the relation of the poem to its author. And I hinted, by an analogy, that the mind of the mature poet differs from that of the immature one not precisely in any valuation of personality, not being necessarily more interesting, or having "more to say," but rather by being a more finely perfected medium in which special, or very varied, feelings are at liberty to enter into new combinations.

The analogy was that of the catalyst. When the two gases previously mentioned are mixed in the presence of a filament of platinum, they form sulphurous acid. This combination takes place only if the platinum is present; nevertheless, the newly formed acid contains no trace of platinum, and the platinum itself is apparently unaffected: has remained inert, neutral, and unchanged. The mind of the poet is the shred of platinum. It may partly or exclusively operate upon the experience of the man himself; but, the more perfect the artist, the more completely separate in him will be the man who suffers and the mind which creates; the more perfectly will the mind digest and transmute the passions which are its material.

—T. S. Eliot, "Tradition and the Individual Talent" (1919), in *Selected Prose of T. S. Eliot*, ed. Frank Kermode (London: Faber and Faber, 1975), 40–1.

GRAHAM HOUGH ON *THE WASTE LAND*'S LACK OF UNITY

[Graham Hough (b. 1908) was Professor of English at Cambridge University and is the author of several books, including *The Dark Sun: A Study of D. H. Lawrence* (1957) and *The Last Romantics* (1949). In this extract from *Reflections on a Literary Revolution* (1960), Hough addresses the question of what unifies the mixed modes of discourse in *The Waste Land*.]

But the questions remain—above all the question of what really makes the poem a totality, if it is one at all. If we can imagine some ideal critic, acquainted with the poetical tradition of Europe, yet innocent of the spirit of our age, and if we can imagine ourselves persuading him to leave the question of total structure in abeyance, "to allow the images to fall into his memory successively without questioning the reasonableness of each"—he would still be struck by the extraordinary rhetorical incongruities. He would find within its four hundred lines passages that are narrative, others that are dramatic, descriptive, lyric, hallucinatory and allusive. The theory of genres was never watertight or exhaustive, but never before was there a poem of this length, or perhaps of any other length, in which the modes were so mixed. Nor is the rhetorical level any more constant than the rhetorical mode. A modern and highly individual elegiac intensity, pastiche Renaissance grandeur, sharp antithetical social comment in the Augustan manner, the low mimetic of public house conversation—all these and probably several other styles are found side by side. The relation of these is sometimes obvious; it is one of calculated contrast. But it is a question how hard such contrasts of texture can be worked in a relatively short poem without disastrous damage to the unity of surface. It is not so much in the obvious collisions of the high and the low styles that this is felt. That kind of calculated shock action is a limited effect, and the intention of producing the shock itself provides a medium between the two elements. It is the use of language in different and unrelated fashions in different parts of the poem that is disruptive. There is the lovely, romantically evocative manner of the hyacinth girl passage [. . .][lines 37–41]. These lines live unhappily in the same poem with [lines 237–42]. [. . .]

The uneasiness does not arise from incompatibility of tone and feeling, but because the two passages are using language in utterly different ways; the first to evoke, by overtones and connotations, the trembling ghost of an intense emotion that is never located or defined; the second to define a situation by precise denotation and intelligent analysis. It is as though a painter were to employ a pointilliste technique in one part of a picture, and the glazes of the high renaissance in another. [. . .]

It has been said that the poem adopts a "stream of consciousness" technique; and this sounds reassuring without committing us to anything very much. But it is precisely what the poem does not do. The advantage of the "stream of consciousness" technique is that it allows a flood of images, more or less emancipated from narrative or logical continuity, while still preserving a psychological continuity—the continuity of inhering in a single consciousness. *The Waste Land* conspicuously foregoes this kind of unifying principle. One desperate expedient has been to fasten on Mr. Eliot's note to line 218: "Tiresias, although a mere spectator and not indeed a 'character,' is yet the most important personage in the poem, uniting all the rest. . . .What Tiresias *sees*, in fact, is the substance of the poem." In the light of this it can be suggested that the whole poem is Tiresias's "stream of consciousness." This is probably to give the note more weight than it can bear, and in any case, it does little to the purpose. Who was Tiresias? A man who had also been a woman, who lived forever and could foretell the future. That is to say, not a single human consciousness, but a mythological catch-all, and as a unifying factor of no effect whatever.

I should like to commit myself to the view that for a poem to exist as a unity more than merely bibliographical, we need the sense of one voice speaking, as in lyric or elegiac verse; or of several voices intelligibly related to each other, as in narrative with dialogue or drama; that what these voices say needs a principle of connection no different from that which would be acceptable in any other kind of discourse; that the collocation of images is not a method at all, but the negation of method. In fact, to expose oneself completely, I want to say that a poem, internally considered, ought to make the same kind of sense as any other discourse.

—Graham Hough, *Reflections on a Literary Revolution* (Washington, DC: The Catholic University of America Press, 1960), 30–5.

NORTHROP FRYE ON CHRISTIAN
REDEMPTION IN *THE WASTE LAND*

[Northrop Frye (1912–1991) taught at the University of
Toronto and was a highly influential critic and theorist. He is
best known for his archetypal criticism, especially as
described in *Anatomy of Criticism* (1957). Among his other
influential books are *Fearful Symmetry* (1947), on William
Blake's visionary symbolism, and *The Great Code* (1982),
about the Bible in the Western tradition. In this extract, Frye
reads *The Waste Land* as a vision of the decline of Europe.]

The Waste Land is a vision of Europe, mainly of London, at the end
of the First World War, and is the climax of Eliot's "infernal" vision.
It appeared in 1922, just before the poet had reached thirty–five, the
middle of life's journey, when Dante began the *Inferno*. The setting is
civilization in the winter of its discontent, and the images are those
of the end of the natural cycle: winter, the "brown land," ruins
(including the nursery-rhyme collapse of London Bridge and, in the
notes, the proposed demolition of nineteen city churches), and the
Thames flowing to the sea. This world is physically above ground
but spiritually subterranean, a world of shadows, corpses and buried
seeds. The inhabitants live the "buried life" (a phrase from "Portrait
of a Lady") of seeds in winter: they await the spring rains resentfully,
for real life would be their death. Human beings who live like seeds,
egocentrically, cannot form a community but only an aggregate,
where "Each man fixed his eyes before his feet," imprisoned in a spiritual solitude that recalls the story of the death of Ugolino in Dante.
Such lines as "And if it rains, a closed car at four" associate human
life with its vegetative metaphors.

Dante's journey through hell begins on Good Friday evening, and
he emerges on the other side of the earth on Easter Sunday morning.
Thus his journey fits inside the three-day rhythm of the redemption,
where Christ is buried on Friday evening, descends to hell on Sat-
urday, and rises on Sunday morning. Similarly in the first section of
The Waste Land, "The Burial of the Dead," we sink into the lower
world of the "unreal city," crowds streaming into it like the damned
in Dante. Here Christ appears as Isaiah's "shadow of a rock in a
weary land," before we descend to the shades below, or as the possible power of resurrection in Ezekiel's valley of dry bones. We

remain in the underworld all through the next two sections, and then follows "Death by Water," evidently physical death, as burial in earth symbolises the physical life which is spiritual death. Physical death is the final judgment between the seeds who can understand the commands of the thunder and die to a new life, and those who merely die and are rejected, as the sterile seed is rejected by nature. The last section repeats the image of a streaming crowd, "hooded hordes swarming," an apocalypse in which the invisible presence of the risen Christ accompanies scenes of terror and chaos as the valley of dry bones becomes "an exceeding great army," as Ezekiel says. [...]

In *The Waste Land* the coming of Christianity represents the turning of Classical culture from its winter into a new spring, for the natural cycle is also associated with the cycles of civilisation. This may be one reason for the prominence of the poets, Virgil and Ovid, who were contemporary with Christ. Whatever future faces us today would, then, logically be connected with a second coming of Christ. The second coming, however, is not a future but a present event, a confronting of man with an immediate demand for self-surrender, sympathy and control, virtues which are primarily social and moral and are preliminary to the Christian faith, hope and love. The London churches, St. Magnus Martyr, St. Mary Woolnoth, and others, stand like sentinels to testify to the presence of the risen Christ in the ruins of Europe.

—Northrop Frye, *T. S. Eliot* (New York: Capricorn Books, 1963), 64–5, 68.

RICHARD ELLMANN ON EZRA POUND'S EDITING OF *THE WASTE LAND* MANUSCRIPT

[Richard Ellmann (b. 1918) was a literary biographer and Professor of English at Emory University and Oxford. His books include biographies of W. B. Yeats (1865–1939), James Joyce (1882–1941) and Oscar Wilde (1854–1900). In this extract, Ellmann presents some of the passages that

Pound advised Eliot to cut from the poem, and describes how their omission was an improvement.]

In its early version *The Waste Land* was woven out of more kinds of material, and was therefore less grave and less organized. The first two sections had an overall title (each had its own title as well), "He Do the Police in Different Voices," a quotation from *Our Mutual Friend*. Dickens has the widow Higden say to her adopted child, "Sloppy is a beautiful reader of a newspaper. He do the Police in different voices." Among the many voices in the first version, Eliot placed at the very beginning a long conversational passage describing an evening on the town, starting at "Tom's place" (a rather arch use of his own name), moving on to a brothel, and concluding with a bathetic sunrise:

> First we had a couple of feelers down at Tom's place,
> There was old Tom, boiled to the eyes, blind . . .
> —("I turned up an hour later down at Myrtle's place.
> What d'y' mean, she says, at two o'clock in the morning,
> I'm not in business here for guys like you;
> We've only had a raid last week, I've been warned twice . . .
> So I got out to see the sunrise, and walked home.

This vapid prologue Eliot decided, apparently on his own, to expunge, and went straight into the now familiar beginning of the poem.

Other voices were expunged by Eliot's friend Ezra Pound, who called himself the "sage homme" (male mid-wife) of the poem. [. . .]

Pound's criticism of *The Waste Land* was not of its meaning; he liked its despair and was indulgent of its neo-Christian hope. He dealt instead with its stylistic adequacy and freshness. For example, there was an extended, unsuccessful imitation of "The Rape of the Lock" at the beginning of "The Fire Sermon." It described the lady Fresca (imported to the waste land from "Gerontion" and one day to be exported to the States for the soft drink trade). Instead of making her toilet like Pope's Belinda, Fresca is going to it, like Joyce's Bloom. Pound warned Eliot that since Pope had done the couplets better, and Joyce the defecation, there was no point in another round. To this shrewd advice we are indebted for the disappearance of such lines as:

The white-armed Fresca blinks, and yawns, and gapes,
Aroused from dreams of love and pleasant rapes.
Electric summons of the busy bell
Brings brisk Amanda to destroy the spell . . .
Leaving the bubbling beverage to cool,
Fresca slips softly to the needful stool,
Where the pathetic tale of Richardson
Eases her labour till the deed is done . . .
This ended, to the steaming bath she moves,
Her tresses fanned by little flutt'ring Loves;
Odours, confected by the cunning French,
Disguise the good old hearty female stench.

The episode of the typist was originally much longer and more laborious:

A bright kimono wraps her as she sprawls
In nerveless torpor on the window seat;
A touch of art is given by the false
Japanese print, purchased in Oxford Street.

Pound found the décor difficult to believe: "Not in that Lodging house?" The stanza was removed. When he read the later stanza,

—Bestows one final patronising kiss,
And gropes his way, finding the stairs unlit;
And at the corner where the stable is,
Delays only to urinate, and spit,

he warned that the last two lines were "probably over the mark," and Eliot acquiesced by cancelling them.

Pound persuaded Eliot also to omit a number of poems that were for a time intended to be placed between the poem's sections, then at the end of it. One was a renewed thrust at poor Bleistein, drowned now but still haplessly Jewish and luxurious under water:

Full fathom five your Bleistein lies
Under the flatfish and the squids.

Graves' Disease in a dead jew's/man's eyes!
Where the crabs have eat the lids . . .

That is lace that was his nose . . .

Roll him gently side to side,
See the lips unfold unfold

From the teeth, gold in gold . . .

Pound urged that this, and several other mortuary poems, did not add anything, either to *The Waste Land* or to Eliot's previous work. He had already written "the longest poem in the English language. Don't try to bust all records by prolonging it three pages further." As a result of this resmithying by *il miglior fabbro*, the poem gained immensely in concentration.

—Richard Ellmann, "The First *Waste Land*," *Eliot in His Time* (Princeton: Princeton University Press, 1973), 53–6.

A. WALTON LITZ ON ELIOT'S NOTES TO *THE WASTE LAND*

[A. Walton Litz is Professor of English at Princeton University and the author of several books of criticism, including important studies of James Joyce, William Carlos Williams, Wallace Stevens, Eliot, and Pound. In this extract, Litz presents Eliot's "retraction" of the notes and argues that they are nonetheless important to understanding the poem's development.]

When *The Waste Land* was first published in magazine form in the autumn of 1922 it was free of annotation: the notes to the poem were added—according to Ezra Pound—at the express wish of the first book publisher, Liveright, who "wanted a longer volume and the notes were the only available unpublished matter." Evidently Eliot's attitude toward the entire apparatus of references and sources, like that of most of his readers, was ambiguous from the start. The fundamental notes were never, of course, a hoax or a publisher's gimmick; they existed in private form during the writing of the poem, and were used by Eliot's friends as *The Waste Land* circulated in typescript. In this sense, the original notes were an integral part of the poem. [. . .]

In his 1956 lecture on "The Frontiers of Criticism" (later published in *On Poetry and Poets*) Eliot made his best-known comment on the notes, a comment remarkable both for its distortion of the original circumstances and for its implication that only the critics have been led into temptation, while the initiated—Eliot's fellow poets—have known how to handle the information.

"Here I must admit that I am, on one conspicuous occasion, not guiltless of having led critics into temptation. The notes to *The Waste Land*! I had at first intended only to put down all the references for my quotations, with a view to spiking the guns of critics of my earlier poems who had accused me of plagiarism. Then, when it came to print *The Waste Land* as a little book—for the poem on its first appearance in *The Dial* and in *The Criterion* had no notes whatever—it was discovered that the poem was inconveniently short, so I set to work to expand the notes, in order to provide a few more pages of printed matter, with the result that they became the remarkable exposition of bogus scholarship that is still on view today. I have sometimes thought of getting rid of these notes; but now they can never be unstuck. They have had almost greater popularity than the poem itself—anyone who bought my book of poems, and found that the notes to *The Waste Land* were not in it, would demand his money back. But I don't think that these notes did any harm to other poets. . . ."

The "bogus scholarship" Eliot refers to is easily identified by any scholar from his own experience: the lengthy quotation from Ovid, in the original Latin; the passage from *Chapman's Handbook of Birds of Eastern North America*; the reference to a pamphlet on *The Proposed Demolition of Nineteen City Churches*—these and similar references are the devices we all use from time to time to dress up or pad out our own work, and they have led to the notion that Eliot's notes are a parody of scholarship (the apparatus of *The Waste Land* so infuriated William Carlos Williams that he could think of *Paterson* as "a reply to Greek and Latin with the bare hands"). Many of the notes *are* "bogus," but only in their lack of proportion. As I shall illustrate in a few moments, every detail in the notes—no matter how trivial—refers to some stage in the imaginative growth of the poem. The problem is not whether to accept or reject the information, but how to weigh and use it. This is exactly the problem Eliot is getting at, obliquely, in "The Frontiers of Criticism," which might have been subtitled: "An attempt to establish sensible frontiers for criticism of *The Waste Land*."

—A. Walton Litz, *The Waste Land Fifty Years After, Eliot in His Time* (Princeton: Princeton University Press, 1973), 8–11.

ELEANOR COOK ON CITIES OF EXILES

[Eleanor Cook is Professor of English at the University of Toronto and an important scholar of literary allusiveness. She is the author of *Poetry, Word-Play and Word-War in Wallace Stevens* (1988). In this essay, Cook maps *The Waste Land*'s apocalyptic mode and describes how the geography of the poem juxtaposes London and Rome.]

In an apocalyptic mode, the world may seem split into the sweetness of a visionary, ideal and virtually unattainable world, and the sordidness of an actual, present, and virtually inescapable world. There is no middle ground, and practical, temporal concerns and governance are left to others. This kind of painful contrast is what gives *The Waste Land* its poignancy. It is the viewpoint of someone not at home in the world, a peregrine, like Augustine. Augustine was an outsider in more than one sense: not only was his overwhelming allegiance given to another world, but he was a provincial in the Roman Empire, one of the *peregrini* or resident aliens during his stay in Milan. In *The Waste Land*, he takes his place among those other great exiles or provincials who perhaps understood their city and their empire all the better for having been exiles or provincials: Ezekiel, Ovid, Dante. And Eliot? One of Eliot's quotations is from the psalm of exile, with its passionate love of Jerusalem, and its cry, "How shall we sing the Lord's song in a strange land?" The cry echoes behind the homeless voices of *The Waste Land*.

But the Jewish voices were able to utter this psalm or to include an Ezekiel. In the twentieth century, there remain only fragmented voices, a desiccated Sibyl. The apocalyptic mode in *The Waste Land* moves toward its own destruction in the disintegration of the uses of language. Augustine, whose etymology is highly idiosyncratic, thought that the name Babylon was connected with the name Babel. Babylon may thus also be called "confusion," and "punishment in the form of a change of language" is the fate of a Babel or of any Babylon or of any Rome—a punishment which some readers may feel Eliot demonstrates with peculiar force. (Another twentieth-century example of this punishment had been seen at the Peace Conference, where the difficulties of negotiating had been compounded by the fact that only Clemenceau, among the Four, spoke both French and English.)

The dangers of abandoning the middle ground of practical, temporal affairs are all too apparent. At the end of *The Waste Land*, there is a turning, or rather a returning, toward this middle earth, and away from exile or private grief. The apocalyptic mode is useful, but not for long. It provides an ideal, but no working pattern for living in this world. A working pattern without an ideal may very well collapse sooner or later, but an ideal with no working pattern can find terrible ways to translate itself into action, or can find itself readily outmanoeuvred and paralysed. Augustine does not ignore the question of how to live in the earthly city. And Keynes, at the end of *The Economic Consequences of the Peace,* tempers his own dark vision with practical suggestions for relieving the nightmare.

The Waste Land, in the end, retains its geographical unity, but the unity becomes far more complex. London as a city forms one focal point. The maps shift, as we muse on the poem, and London becomes a center of empire, another Rome. Do they ever shift again, so that London and Rome become Jerusalem, the center of Dante's world? Never, in the old sense, and not until *Little Gidding* in a mystical sense, and by this time the center may be anywhere. "England and nowhere. Never and always."

—Eleanor Cook, "T. S. Eliot and the Carthaginian Peace," *ELH* 46 (1979): 353–4.

CLEO MCNELLY KEARNS ON ELIOT'S RESPONSE TO WHITMAN

[Cleo McNelly Kearns (b. 1943) teaches English at Rutgers University and is the author of *T. S. Eliot and Indic Traditions* (1987). In this extract, Kearns considers Eliot's difficult discipleship with Whitman, who presented for him not only a troubling sexual politics but a problematic vision of poetry at the boundary of Eastern and Western thought.]

Eliot was able fully to admit the greatness of Whitman, however, only after he had to come to terms with his own American identity and achieved that poetic mastery on his own terms which gave him the security to confront his precursor again. The problem was clearly one of influence in the Bloomian sense, and Eliot often put it in just these terms. During the course of an essay called "American Literature and American Language" written in 1953 (in *To Criticize the Critic*) Eliot took up the question of influence explicitly, and he did so, significantly, in the context of a consideration of Whitman, Twain, and Poe. For models to *imitate*, Eliot said, a writer will often go to (usually minor) writers of another country and another language. By contrast, the great writers of the immediate past in his own tradition will function largely as "something definite to rebel against." There is a distinction, however, Eliot went on to argue, between genuine "influence" and the imitation of models or styles. "A true disciple is impressed by what his master has to say," he wrote, "and *consequently* by his way of saying it; an imitator—I might say a borrower—is impressed chiefly by the way his master said it." In this sense, Eliot was an "imitator" or "borrower" from the French, but he was a *disciple* of the Americans, and particularly of Whitman. Furthermore, by his own testimony, his discipleship had to do primarily with "what Whitman had to say" and only consequently with "how he said it."

"What Whitman had to say" involved [. . .] both radical democracy and sexual politics, and it also involved, crucially for Eliot, a certain very distinct, cogent and challenging reading of Eastern thought. While he seems to have been innocent of very much direct contact with Eastern texts, and innocent as well of the kinds of epistemological despair that they raised in both earlier and later orientalists, Whitman had nevertheless achieved, by his maturity, a remarkable, original and culturally prescient understanding of one tendency in the Eastern traditions. That understanding, as recent critics of the relation between American and Hindu thought have increasingly stressed (V. K. Chari, Beongcheon Yu), was highly realist in terms of its Western orientation, rather than representing in a familiar way the philosophical idealism to which Eastern texts are more frequently assimilated in the West. Whitman's importance for Eliot, then, certainly lay in his understanding, inherent in the *Bhagavad Gita*, among other texts, but often overlooked there, of a detached but affirmative relation to sense experience, of an exoteric and culturally open approach to philosophical and religious truth, and of the validity of the active as well as the contemplative life. Eliot was never more Whitman's "disciple" than in his ability to envision in Eastern texts something more compelling, more disturbing and ultimately more liberating than mere denunciations of the world of appearance as pure illusion. [...]

In his relation to Whitman, seen in the context of the thought of [Bertrand] Russell, and indeed of the upanishadic tradition as well, Eliot seeks, before our half-horrified, half-enamoured eyes, to cross the gap or abyss that separates the radical democrat from the Gallic poseur, the sexually free from the sexually contorted or repressed, the poetically accessible and fraternal from the poetically Oedipal and closed, the esoteric and philosophically idealist from the exoteric and realist position. That chasm cannot be easily traversed, and only in recognition of its depth can we make any sense at all of the contradictions in Eliot's work. Eliot's early career, more than that of any other modernist, dramatizes the difficult problem of translation involved when we seek to turn a mental and philosophical image of liberation into the objective reality of political, sexual, and aesthetic release.

—Cleo McNelly Kearns, "Eliot, Russell, and Whitman: Realism, Politics, and Literary Persona in *The Waste Land*," *T. S. Eliot's The Waste Land*, ed. Harold Bloom, (New York: Chelsea House Publishers, 1986): 145–6, 152.

Thematic Analysis of
"The Hollow Men"

First published in 1925, "The Hollow Men" addresses failures of human courage and faith. More simply worded but in some ways more obscure than Eliot's earlier work, the poem innovatively combines minimalist techniques Eliot inherited from Pound's Imagism with choruses reminiscent of Greek tragedy.[1] Its effects rely on indirect images and subtle rhythmic variations, techniques that make the poem more a matter of suggestiveness than statement. The two epigraphs suggest underlying themes and deeply submerged narrative sources. The first epigraph, "Mistah Kurtz—he dead," is from Joseph Conrad's *Heart of Darkness*, a story about the exploration of the Congo that examines the hollowness and horror of lack of faith, spiritual paralysis, and despair. "The Hollow Men" powerfully displays what Hugh Kenner calls Eliot's affinity with "Conrad's vision of subtle evisceration."[2]

The second epigraph, "A penny for the Old Guy," refers to the celebration of Guy Fawkes Day in Britain. In 1605, in what came to be known as the Gunpowder Plot, conspirators seeking retaliation for persecution of Catholics plotted to blow up the Parliament building with King James I, his family, and his ministers inside. Guy Fawkes, one of the leaders of the assassination attempt, was discovered in the cellar where the gunpowder was being stored, and the plot was foiled. Under torture, Fawkes named his co-conspirators, and all were either killed while trying to escape or executed. A day of public thanksgiving for rebellion thwarted, November fifth is celebrated with bonfires, fireworks, the burning of scarecrows, and solicitation of "pennies for the Old Guy." Eliot's images of scarecrows, a cellar, and violent souls recall this tale of a violent plot that ended, not with a bang, but with an act of cowardice.

Another story of violent actions undertaken on high principles, Shakespeare's *Julius Caesar* is a third important source for the poem. The title "The Hollow Men" echoes Brutus's speech in which he expresses concern about the insincerity of his allies in conspiracy, calling them hollow men (*Julius Caesar* IV.ii.23).[3]

Part I opens with the chant-like chorus of "the hollow men ... the stuffed men." Like scarecrows, these empty effigies are puffed up, lacking embodiment or substance. Their collaboration produces only a whisper of "dried voices" that is "quiet and meaningless," likened to "wind in dry grass" and "rats' feet over broken glass / In our dry cellar." The images recall the Gunpowder Plot and also convey a general sense of desolation. In the monotone of this collective voice, no one speaks up: as "shape without form, shade without colour, / Paralysed force, gesture without motion," they are trapped by depression and indolence, drained of any vitality.

Eliot presents the Hollow Men as resembling souls in Dante's Ante-Hell of Neutrals (*Inferno* III), those who died "without disgrace and without praise" and who "commingle with the coward angels," neither faithful nor actively rebellious. The Hollow Men do not deserve the recognition of being "violent souls," and can only watch "those who have crossed . . . to death's other Kingdom." They languish in inaction, forgotten because they were neither good nor evil.

"Eyes" are an important and repeated image of spiritual insight in the poem. In Part II, the Hollow Men, unlike those "with direct eyes," have vision that is refracted and distorted. They do not dare to meet a full-face gaze, but find themselves in "death's dream kingdom," where eyes are "sunlight on a broken column." The image suggests a ruin in a classical landscape painting, a symbol of a broken-down system of belief. Older forms are distant and solemn, and "a fading star" is viewed only from far off. Even if the star represents paradise, as it does in Dante, the Hollow Men wish to keep their distance ("be no nearer") and remain masked and anonymous ("Let me also wear / Such deliberate disguises"). Their disguises suggest identically-suited businessmen, conformists and blind adherents to unexamined codes of behavior. "Crossed staves / in a field" suggest the trees of crucifixion as well as scarecrows' posts. Flaccid forms without substance, the Hollow Men behave "as the wind behaves": they are passive and amoral, acting only in avoidance of a final meeting that would force a confrontation or judgment upon them. The poem critiques this don't-make-waves attitude and its spiritual repercussions.

Some critics have argued that Eliot constructed this poem from *The Waste Land*'s leftover lines, and the arid landscape in Part III resembles the earlier treatment of "dead land." "The Hollow Men" was written, at least in part, several years before its publication, and reflects Eliot's own crises of faith in the period, as well as his struggles with psychological collapse. Eliot revisits this scene of the failure of belief, the worship of graven images, to emphasize its deadness. The distant fading star appears again, but its luminousness has no effect on those whose prayers amount to the "supplication of a dead man's hand." Eliot employs simple prose rhythms throughout the poem, but in this part especially, with phrases like "it is like this," he underscores the banality of the Hollow Men's quotidian composure, composure that is also the source of their despair. They can achieve no human fulfillment: "Lips that would kiss / Form prayers to broken stone." Their prayers are sterile, incapable of issuing solace.

In Part IV, "eyes" of spiritual insight have been lost entirely. In this "valley of dying stars," an image that continues the earlier star motif, faith that was already fading is now almost extinguished. "This broken jaw of our lost kingdoms," with its biblical resonance, suggests that hope for a spiritual kingdom has been fossilized. With its jaw unhinged, prophesy can no longer be uttered. The Hollow Men now "grope together / And avoid speech" in a landscape that is reminiscent of Dante's ante-hell and of *The Waste Land*. At the "tumid" river, their blindness is almost total: they are "sightless / unless the eyes reappear." Some hope remains for transcendence, for consolation in a "perpetual star / Multifoliate rose," another important link to Dante, where a rose symbolizes the epitome of spiritual fulfillment in Paradise. In what Ronald Bush calls a "drama of salvation," the search for a "twilight kingdom" becomes "the hope only / Of empty men."

The Hollow Men's grasping at religious significance leads only to a parody of a nursery rhyme, maniacally chanted. Moreover, they do not even circle a lush and fecund "mulberry bush," but a cactus, a feature of the arid "cactus land" of Part III. The song is then sharply contrasted with the abstract philosophical diction of "between the idea / and the reality." The series of "betweens" situates the Hollow Men in an ambiguous state between idea and reality, motion and act, conception and creation, emotion and response. Between these alternatives "falls the Shadow" an uncrossable gulf that leaves them existentially stuck, caught in the disjunctiveness of their own rhetoric. In an effort to remedy the gap between incommensurables, they appeal to the Lord's Prayer ("For Thine is the Kingdom"), but the attempt is stalled by further effort to address the Shadow. The line "Life is very long," which revises the familiar axiom *ars longa*, *vita brevis* (art is long, life is short), suggests that life without some spiritual answer is hopelessly prolonged.

The third set of "between" statements, less familiar dichotomies with more nebulous significance, suggest that the sexual energies of the life cycle have also been disrupted. The "shadow" imposes a divergence between "desire" and "spasm," "potency" and "existence," "essence" and "descent." As the Hollow Men are spiritually impotent and sterile, they are creatively and pro-creatively empty as well. After the second italicized "For Thine is the Kingdom," the Hollow Men seem to attempt the prayer themselves, but they can utter only fragments. Their inability to complete the prayer, or the thought "Life is . . . ," suggests that they are unable to overcome the "Shadow" of their spiritual inertia. As Kenner points out, the Hollow Men's piety is "a piety of incapacity" (166).

The poem concludes with a chant that seems to accelerate to a climax, the repetition of the line "This is the way the world ends" suggesting increasing urgency. Instead, against our expectations, it peters out. The poem ends with an anticlimax in two senses. Metrically, it ends not with a "bang," a hard stress, but with a "whimper," an unstressed syllable. Thematically, the "world" ends not with explosive intensity but with pathetic sniveling. No cathartic conflagration purges the Hollow Men's sins of omission. In Dante's schema, "hollow men" remain just within the gates of hell—out of the fire, but still damned. In Eliot's, the Hollow Men remain behind their protective masks. ❋

---

[1] Ronald Bush, *T. S. Eliot: A Study in Character and Style* (New York: Oxford University Press, 1983), 93, 97–8.
[2] Hugh Kenner, *The Invisible Poet: T. S. Eliot* (London: W. H. Allen, 1960), 159.
[3] For more details about the sources of this poem, see B. C. Southam, *A Student's Guide to the Selected Poems of T. S. Eliot* (Boston: Faber and Faber, 1990), 148–63.

Critical Views on
"The Hollow Men"

HELEN GARDNER ON THE DIFFICULTY OF READING ELIOT

[Helen Gardner (b. 1908) was a scholar of Modernist poetry and also wrote studies of Milton, Shakespeare, and the Metaphysical poets. In this extract, Gardner addresses the common frustration with Eliot's obscure references and difficult style and discusses how the modern poet, especially a religious one, has certain problems of communication.]

The problem of communication for a religious poet in an age where his religious beliefs are not widely held is a special aspect of the general problem of communication for the poet in the modern world. Until about a hundred years ago the public for whom a poet wrote was, if not so compact and unified culturally as is sometimes suggested, at least in rough agreement as to what an educated man should be presumed to know. Obviously not all the courtiers who listened to Chaucer reading his poems, nor all the readers for whom Caxton printed *The Canterbury Tales* can have been aware of the width of Chaucer's reading, or recognized the varied sources he was drawing on; but the kind of learning Chaucer had—in the classics, in old and new medieval poetry, in the discipline of rhetoric—was the kind of learning expected of a poet; a kind of learning to which educated men aspired. In the same way not all Milton's readers can have recognized all his classical allusions, or been able to complete at once the story of a myth he referred to in passing, but in general his readers regarded Greek and Latin poetry as the proper study in schools and universities. If, among familiar allusions, there were some that were remote, the audience did not feel irritated by the poet's superiority in culture. The less well-educated reader, aware that he was less well-educated, did not blame the poet for displaying a deeper knowledge, nor resent his possessing it. The modern poet is in a very different position. The reading public is far larger, the output of printed matter incomparably greater, and the content of education has expanded so enormously that there is now no general cultural tradition to which the poet can refer or be referred. The divisions do not only run between those who are trained in the scientific disciplines and those trained in the humanities; but between science and science and between one branch of the humanities and another. The development of English Literature and Modern Languages as academic subjects has had something to do with making communication more difficult for the modern poet than for his ancestor, for whom the humanities meant Greek and Latin. Many poets have been inspired to a greater or less degree by their reading. The inspiration is not usually sought deliberately; it happens by accidents of education and environment and even more by some need in the individual temperament of the poet. [. . .]

Part of the difficulty of Mr. Eliot's early work arose from what he has described himself as "an intense and narrow taste determined by personal needs." This early taste led him to the later Elizabethan dramatists for a style of great rhetorical force, and to the French symbolists for a manner that allowed him to express an intensely individual view of life with the minimum of direct statement. The personal need was in his temperament—ironic, diffident, at war with his surroundings; sceptical, preferring understatement, hints and suggestions; fastidious, reserved, acutely sensitive to beauty and ugliness, but even more to misery and happiness. [. . .]

We have, I need hardly say, no right to complain of a poet's being difficult and to insist that he must be comprehensible to the average reader without any special trouble. Nor is being difficult a merit in itself. We have to read poetry on the poet's own terms, and the poet is perfectly at liberty to write if he chooses for "fit audience though few," just as the reader is perfectly at liberty not to read him. There have always been difficult poets, though they have not always been met with the same hostility as is shown to them today, when the difficult poet is blamed for superiority rather than admired for ingenuity.

—Helen Gardner, *The Art of T. S. Eliot* (New York: Dutton, 1950), 68–9, 70, 72.

HUGH KENNER ON THE HOLLOW MEN AS LOST SOULS

[Hugh Kenner taught at the Johns Hopkins University and Emory University. He is the leading critic of Eliot and other High Modernists, including Pound and Joyce. Among his books are *The Pound Era* (1971), *Flaubert, Joyce, Beckett: The Stoic Comedians* (1962), and *The Invisible Poet: T. S. Eliot* (1960) from which this extract is taken. Kenner interprets "The Hollow Men" as a poem of "personal inertia."]

Hence this chorus of the respectable, condemned, partly by personal inertia and partly by the sanctions of an historic process reaching from the Renaissance, to inhabit "death's dream kingdom," not remembered, to be sure, as "lost violent souls," but, not on the other hand, even memorable. If Tiresias, morbidly fascinated by the behaviour of other people, is the epiphany of an over-knowing inability to respect their inviolate otherness, the Hollow Men, morbidly fascinated by their own lyric inertia, epiphanize the flaccid forbearance of an upper-middleclass twentieth-century community, where no one speaks loudly, and where the possession of an impeccably tailored uniform marks one as unlikely to disturb the silence [. . .] [—]the scarecrow a mock crucifix, the dead rats and crows hung in symbolic admonition to rodent or corvine malefactors, as great sinners were once hung in chains.

In death's dream kingdom, as in the minor lyric verse of the nineteenth century, nothing happens, there are no confrontations [. . .] Hence there are no persons here besides ourselves, who are scarcely persons, only components in a modish surreal landscape by a Berman or a Chirico[.] Death has some other kingdom, about which we can only guess ("Is it like this?"). To death's other kingdom certain persons have crossed "with direct eyes," "absolute for death," as the Duke said in *Measure for Measure*; but "there are no eyes here." And the reappearance here of eyes, corresponding to the assertion of a new iconography, not broken columns and stone images but "the perpetual star, multifoliate rose," is, by a profound ambivalence,

> The hope only
> Of empty men.

Men who have emptied themselves—for "the soul cannot be possessed on the divine union, until it has divested itself of the love of created beings" —are entitled to hope for this metamorphosis of symbols. For the empty men who parody those saints it is only a hope, and a forlorn one.

"The Hollow Men" parody the saints; in this poem Eliot first ventures on the structural principle of all his later work: the articulation of moral states which to an external observer are indistinguishable from one another, but which in their interior dynamics parody one another. We can judge a man's actions, but we cannot judge the man by his actions. In art, in drama, actions are determined by their motives, which are hidden: hidden, often, from the actor.[. . .] So the hollow men go round the prickly pear, wearing "deliberate disguises," though there is no sign that their pasts contain any action that requires justifying. There is also no sign to the contrary; it is precisely the index to their state, that what was done or undone in the past is irrelevant to it; that activity is irrelevant to it, and motive irrelevant to it; that like the souls in Paradise they inhabit a state which, however they came to merit it, is now that they have entered it immune from considerations of merit, of sequence and consequence. Their world of sunlight, a swinging tree and distant solemn voices parodies that of the blessed souls. The damned, as Dante discovered, tirelessly rehearse the irrevocable sequence of activities that brought them to damnation; and in purgatory a soul passes the stages of its age and youth; but heaven and the dream kingdom alike are timeless states untouched by any memory of time.

—Hugh Kenner, *The Invisible Poet: T. S. Eliot* (London: W. H. Allen, 1960), 161–4.

SIR HERBERT READ ON POETRY AND BELIEF

[Sir Herbert Read (1893–1968) was a British art historian, poet, and man of letters. Among his books are *Art and Society* (1936), *The Philosophy of Modern Art* (1952) and *The True Voice of Feeling: Studies in English Romantic Poetry* (1953). In this extract, Read sees "The Hollow Men" as a poem of religious crisis that represents the end of Eliot's "pure poetry." Belief, Read argues, is not incompatible with poetry, but a traditional system of dogma and moral commands "stultified" Eliot's poetic powers.]

The most significant of all Eliot's poems, from a confessional point of view, is "The Hollow Men". It was written in 1925, the year of religious crisis, and apart from some minor poems, it is the last example of what I would call his *pure* poetry. *Ash–Wednesday*, which followed in 1930, is already a moralistic poem, especially in the last two sections. All the poetry that follows, including the *Four Quartets*, is, in spite of flashes of the old fire, moralistic poetry.

There are no strict rules for the creation of poetry, but nevertheless a poem is neither an arbitrary nor a deliberate event. As critics we must act on the assumption that a correspondence exists between the shifting levels of consciousness and what we call moments of vision or flashes of inspiration. One of the critic's tasks is to survey the devious intercommunications between these various levels of consciousness. So long as the lines of communication are open, inspiration, as we say, *flows*. For a time, for a year or perhaps five years, rarely more than ten, the divine madness, as Plato called it, descends on a mortal and then burns out. "The Hollow Men" is a celebration of this incineration. "Mistah Kurtz—he dead. A penny for the Old Guy." But Mistah Kurtz, though he may have been a bad man, a corrupt man, a suffering man, saw visions that were splendid. Even when, as in this poem, he is evoking "death's other Kingdom," he does so in bright images, "Sunlight on a broken column," "a tree swinging"; but then, alas, "Between the emotion/And the response/Falls the Shadow." What Eliot meant by the Shadow is clear enough and it is not a Shadow that we encounter in his poetry without sorrow. [...]

[The] distinction between dogma and belief would allow us to assume that belief is a process of psychic integration, precariously maintained. As such it need not conflict with poetic intuition, which is also a delicate process of psychic integration. In this both belief and poetry differ from those inflexible moral commands to which a man must, if he resigns his life and would have peace, assent. This was made clear by Pascal, and by Unamuno in *The Agony of Christianity*. The Jesuits, we are told, do not ask for faith but for obedience; and Unamuno suggests that it was such a demand that led Pascal, in a moment of fear, to cry: *It will stultify you.* (*Cela vous abêtira.*) The fragmented conclusion of "The Hollow Men" is the same cry of despair, the same broken utterance:

> For Thine is
> Life is
> For Thine is the

Perhaps the key to Eliot's agony lies in this essay on Pascal; his was the same agony as Pascal's, but I think that in the end Eliot resigned his life for that life, *stultified his speech* for that unspoken law. Pascal, he said, was to be commended "to those who doubt, but who have the mind to conceive, and the sensibility to feel, the disorder, the futility, the meaninglessness, the mystery of life and suffering, and who can only find peace through a satisfaction of the whole being." Eliot himself, I believe, was not one of those who doubt, but rather one of those great mystics who, in his words, "like St. John of the Cross, are primarily for readers with a special determination of purpose."

I am not trying to suggest that there is any incompatibility between the religious *belief* of a man like Eliot and his poetic *practice*—how could I with the examples of George Herbert and the later Donne to prove the contrary, not to mention Dante? But a problem does exist for the poet who has "a special determination of purpose"; such a phrase implies a process of rationalization, by which we mean a conscious justification of dogma and morals as distinct from beliefs that are essentially irrational or instinctive. The habit of rationalization sustains the mystic, but it is a deadly habit in the poet.

—Sir Herbert Read, "T. S. E.—A Memoir," in *T. S. Eliot: The Man and His Work*, ed. Allen Tate (New York: Delacorte Press, 1966), 34–7.

B. C. SOUTHAM ON ELIOT'S USE OF DANTE

[B. C. Southam is the author of *A Student's Guide to the Selected Poems of T. S. Eliot* (1990), from which this extract is taken. In "The Hollow Men," Southam argues, Eliot's "kingdoms" refer to Dante's "allegorical dream-visions" in the *Divine Comedy*.]

(*iii*) Eliot's use of Dante is more indirect and much more important [than any other allusions in the poem]. The three books of the *Divina Commedia* compose an allegorical dream-vision in which Dante himself is conducted through the hell of punishment and of lost souls (in the *Inferno*), the Purgatory of suffering towards redemption (*Purgatorio*), and Paradise, a higher, perfect world of beauty, light and music (*Paradiso*). Putting the matter very arbitrarily, it can be said that the condition of the hollow men is that of the lost souls in Hell. They are the inhabitants of "death's dream kingdom" gathered at their last meeting-place beside a "tumid river" (lines 57–60). In Dante, this corresponds to the scene beside the River Acheron (*Inferno* iii) where the spirits of the damned wait to be ferried across to Hell. There is also another group, which seems to correspond more precisely to Eliot's hollow men. These are the shades which have never been spiritually alive, never experienced good or evil, having lived narrowly for themselves. They are rejected by both Heaven and Hell, and are condemned to stay eternally by the river. Eliot seems to be referring to their condition in lines 11–12. In *The Waste Land* [see note to line 63] Eliot associates them with the crowds crossing London Bridge. In this respect, the hollow men are not narrowly the conspirators; they are all mankind (an interpretation supported by Eliot's use of "Heart of Darkness").

Eliot refers to a second kingdom, "death's other kingdom." If "death's dream kingdom" is related to the fallen, sinful world of the *Inferno* and *Purgatorio*, this second kingdom is related to the Paradiso, and the aspect of this perfect world which Dante glimpses in the closing books of the *Purgatorio*. Here we read of Dante's arrival at the summit of the Mount of Purgatory, at the top of which is the Earthly Paradise, the Garden of Eden where he meets Beatrice, formerly his beloved on earth, now a figure of blessedness, spiritual beauty, and revelation. Section II of Eliot's poem is concerned with the courage and self-scrutiny which are needed even to catch a glimpse of that vision.

There is a third kingdom, "death's twilight kingdom" (lines 38, 65). This seems to be a transitional stage between the "dream" and the "other" kingdoms. In Dante, it corresponds with the poet's progress towards Beatrice in the Earthly Paradise. He has first to Pass through the River Lethe, which flows in shadow, then through the River Eunoë; the first river washes away all memory of sin, the second restores the memory of righteousness. It is a stage at which Dante is humbled and shamed by the memory of his sins and unfaithfulness to Beatrice. In the scheme of Eliot's poem, this "twilight kingdom" is the condition in which man has to face the truth about himself and life, as Kurtz does [. . .] The fourth kingdom is the kingdom of God, which can be spoken of only in broken words (see line 77).

—B. C. Southam, *A Student's Guide to the Selected Poems of T. S. Eliot* (Boston: Faber and Faber, 1990), 150–1.

Thematic Analysis of
"Journey of the Magi"

In 1927, Geoffrey Faber, head of the publishing house where Eliot worked, approached him about contributing poems to a series of illustrated pamphlets for the Christmas season. Directed toward a fairly broad audience, each pamphlet would present a single poem. Eliot, eager to break a period of "writer's block" that had followed *The Hollow Men,* agreed, and four poems followed: "Journey of the Magi," "A Song for Simeon," "Animula," and "Marina."[1] All four poems address aspects of rebirth.

Written after Eliot's conversion, this first "Ariel poem" addresses an explicitly religious theme, the New Testament account (from the Gospel of Matthew 2:1–12) of the Magi, the three "wise men" or astrologers from the East, sometimes characterized as priests of ancient Persia, who come to adore the infant Jesus. The poem is a dramatic monologue spoken in the voice of one of the Magi, who relates the journey with matter-of-fact, prose-like clarity. The images are not always straightforward, however, and present a complex array of descriptive and prophetic elements that allude to Christian mysteries. Eliot addresses, in Peter Ackroyd's terms, the theme of "the painful necessity of rebirth which is itself a form of 'Death,' creating weariness and suffering—as well as a sense of alienation among men . . ." (164). Eliot addresses the birth of Christ as an event that is at once commonplace and momentous, altering the fates of the human subjects involved as well as the forces of history and civilization.

The poem begins with a modified quotation from a sermon given by Bishop Lancelot Andrewes in 1622. Eliot greatly admired Andrewes's Nativity Sermons, which were delivered before King James each Christmas Day between 1605 and 1624, for their originality and erudition. (See Eliot's 1926 essay on Andrewes in *Selected Prose*). Eliot adopts Andrewes's directness. Details engage the reader in the unpleasant realities that these determined travelers had to cope with: stubborn camels refusing to go farther ("lying down in melted snow"), impatient and weary camel drivers running off for "liquor and women," and high prices for lodgings. The reader easily identifies with their exasperation. The informal syntax that lists their hardships, the use of the word *and* to suggest one thing piled on top of another, conveys the sense that the Magi are, in contemporary terms, getting fed up. With the image of the "summer palaces," we see the Magi longing for the comforts and luxuries of home, regretting an endeavor of unclear purpose that has taken them so far. They are forced to "travel all night, / Sleeping in snatches," suggesting an urgency and extremity in their situation that brings psychological as well as physical discomfort. "The voices singing in our ears" are their own doubts and the doubts of others, the fear that "this was all folly." They proceed with a journey that intensifies, not mollifies, these doubts.

The second verse-paragraph shifts into longer lines, as if the verse itself relaxes with the Magi's arrival in "a temperate valley." The severity of the climate as well as their travel woes are "tempered" in this region "smelling of vegetation": rebirth is happening here. We are given a travelogue of sorts as the Magi scan the landscape: they are getting close to their destination and can now focus on the foreground of the scene they witness. The images that Eliot presents allude to other biblical accounts, prophetic glimpses of Christ's life to come. The "three trees on the low sky" prefigure the three crosses erected at Golgotha, the site of Christ's crucifixion. The "white horse" suggests the prediction in Revelation (6:2; 19:11–14) that Christ will arrive riding a white horse in the Second Coming. "Six hands at an open door dicing for pieces of silver" alludes to Judas's betrayal of Christ for 30 pieces of silver and the soldiers dicing for his robes after the crucifixion, as recorded in the Gospel of Matthew (26:14–15, 27:35). The image of "feet kicking the empty wine-skins" encapsulates the progress of Christ's earthly career—from the joyful miracle of changing water to wine at Cana to the in-the-gutter public violence of carrying the cross. While all these images resonate with biblical accounts, they are at the same time plausible details of what the Magi see as they approach Bethlehem.

Even in the last segment of their trip, "there was no information," and the Magi must persist with obscure understanding of a dubious prospect. The actual arrival at the scene of the birth is not described, emphasizing the irreproducibility of the revelation itself. They arrive "not a moment too soon," suggesting that the urgency of their journeying was necessary, but the climactic moment is described with a conversational understatement that deflates that urgency: "It was (you may say) satisfactory." The off-hand parenthetical suggests deliberate avoidance of the grandiose or theatrical. Satisfactory is typically used to describe something adequate or average, but hardly wonderful, yet here the word suggests a deeper kind of satisfaction, the Magi wholly satisfied by the event. The miracle has brought an utter and thorough change for the witnesses, but not a great exaltation.

In the third verse-paragraph, Eliot shifts to the "scene of composition," the Magus stating the time and distance that separate him from the event. The Magus acknowledges "I would do it again": they found what they came for, had "evidence and no doubt." But the knowledge they received was bitter: "this Birth was / Hard and bitter agony for us, like Death, our death." In the most emphatic lines of the poem, the Magus insists, "but set down / This set down / This. . . . " He makes a fierce attempt to "get it right." The "this" is not a statement but a question: "were we led all that way for / Birth or Death?" As Christianity formulates them, birth and death are reciprocal processes, making the event bitter for them for two reasons: the central mystery of Christianity requires death to bring eternal life, and it also requires the death of the Magi's old system of belief. When they return to their home, they are alienated from their own people, "no longer at ease here, in the old dispensation." The final line—"I should be glad of another death"—suggests the speaker's longing for the end of his own life, a weariness about the life-shaking event from which he can never return to normalcy.

The poem can be fruitfully compared with W. B. Yeats's "The Magi," published in 1914. As Christianity was the new dispensation, Yeats awaits a *new* "new dispensation," a system of beliefs that is due to replace Christianity and inaugurate a new historical cycle. His Magi are "hoping to find once more, / Being by Calvary's turbulence unsatisfied, / The uncontrollable mystery on the bestial floor." For Yeats, the Christian Incarnation is no longer sufficient. Eliot's account parts company with Yeats's: his Magus sees the mystery as irrevocable and satisfactory, and he can no longer imagine any other system of belief. He finds himself sorrowful among "an alien people clutching their gods": rebirth has left an indelible mark. ❈

[1] See also B. C. Southam (179) and Peter Ackroyd (164–5).

Critical Views on
"Journey of the Magi"

GROVER SMITH ON NEGATION AND ACCEPTANCE

[Grover Smith (b. 1923) was Professor of English at Duke University and is the author of critical studies of Archibald MacLeish, Ford Madox Ford, and T. S. Eliot. In this sensitive analysis, Smith discusses the Magus's resignation to his predicament, trapped between an old world and a new revelation.]

"Journey of the Magi" is the monologue of a man who has made his own choice, who has achieved belief in the Incarnation, but who is still part of that life which the Redeemer came to sweep away. Like Gerontion, he cannot break loose from the past. Oppressed by a sense of death-in-life (Tiresias' anguish "between two lives"), he is content to submit to "another death" for his final deliverance from the world of old desires and gods, the world of "the silken girls." It is not that the Birth that is also Death has brought him hope of a new life, but that it has revealed to him the hopelessness of the previous life. He is resigned rather than joyous, absorbed in the negation of his former existence but not yet physically liberated from it. Whereas Gerontion is "waiting for rain" in this life, and the hollow men desire the "eyes" in the next life, the speaker here has put behind him both the life of the senses and the affirmative symbol of the Child; he has reached the state of desiring nothing. His negation is partly ignorant, for he does not understand in what way the Birth is a Death; he is not aware of the sacrifice. Instead, he himself has become the sacrifice; he has reached essentially, on a symbolic level true to his emotional, if not to his intellectual, life, the humble, negative stage that in a mystical progress would be prerequisite to union. Although in the literal circumstances his will cannot be fixed upon mystical experience, because of the time and condition of his existence, he corresponds symbolically to the seeker as described by St. John of the Cross in *The Ascent of Mount Carmel*. Having first approached the affirmative symbol, or rather, for him, the affirmative reality, he has experienced failure; negation is his secondary option.[. . .]

The arrival of the Magi at the place of Nativity, whose symbolism has been anticipated by the fresh vegetation and the mill "beating the darkness," is only a "satisfactory" experience. The narrator has seen and yet he does not fully understand; he accepts the fact of Birth but is perplexed by its similarity to a Death, and to death which he has seen before [lines 32–36]. Were they led there for Birth or for Death? or, perhaps, for neither? or to make a choice between Birth and Death? And whose Birth or Death was it? their own, or Another's? Uncertainty leaves him mystified and unaroused to the full splendor of the strange epiphany. So he and his fellows have come back to their own Kingdoms, where, [lines 41–42] (which are now alien gods), they linger not yet free to receive "the dispensation of the grace of God." The speaker has reached the end of one world, but despite his acceptance of the revelation as valid, he cannot gaze into a world beyond his own.

—Grover Smith, *T. S. Eliot's Poetry and Plays: A Study in Sources and Meaning* (Chicago: The University of Chicago Press, 1956), 122–4.

RONALD TAMPLIN ON RELIGIOUS VISION

[Ronald Tamplin teaches at the University of Exeter and has published several books and articles on modern poetry, including *A Preface to T. S. Eliot*, from which this extract is taken. Tamplin discusses the difficulty of presenting a visionary climax in a poem about religious witness.]

At this point [line 29] follows, perhaps, the true strangeness of the poem. Up till now the visual has predominated in the poem, but now, at the moment of arrival, the actual sight of Jesus is shrouded. The incarnation in "Gerontion" was treated obscurely through an intellectual conceit and as a report from the Gospel rather than an actual sight. Even so, this most revolutionary moment in history for the Christian was at least given the colour and excitement of tradition. Here the statement is bald, like an official striving to say nothing [lines 29–31]. There is, of course, always the problem of how to present a climactic vision anyway. What the Magi saw was a baby, and, in visual terms, one baby is much like another. There is no easy way to give the description a poise commensurate with its meanings. All the Magi really know is that something happened. As Simeon, the old prophet, says in another *Ariel* poem, "A Song for Simeon:"

> Not for me the ultimate vision. . . .
> Let thy servant depart,
> Having seen thy salvation.

But this is visionary in its language compared with what Eliot allows in "Journey of the Magi." And it may be so because Eliot had no strong incarnational sense of God, and so naturally describes the birth in terms adequate to faith but colourless to feeling. A revealing phrase in this light is "it was (you may say) satisfactory," where "(you may say)" is in some sense an evasion, an allowance to a listener rather than a direct statement. "Satisfactory," surprisingly, is not as colourless as it seems. Rather it is a pun in that Christ's redemptive act of dying on the cross is often seen as an act of satisfaction for the sins of man, "taking the faults of man upon himself" (Hebrews 9.28). It is a technical term for this sufficient act of Christ.

Similarly, the identification of birth and death in the final section can lead to unnecessary confusion. It is a commonplace in any transitional state, any *rite de passage*, as anthropologists call it, to see the change as the death of an old way of life and the birth of a new one. What gives added subtlety and complexity to Eliot's use of the idea is that it involves the actual birth and the anticipated death of Jesus, the initiation (as birth and death) of the Magi and also the anticipated actual death of the narrator. All these levels coalesce in the passage. For instance, in the final line the narrator is anticipating Christ's death so as to complete the process of salvation begun by the birth he has witnessed. Meanwhile, as Eliot so often has been himself, he is at odds with his inheritance, "no longer at ease here, in the old dispensation, / With an alien people clutching their gods."

—Ronald Tamplin, *A Preface to T. S. Eliot* (New York: Longman, 1987), 144–5.

KINERETH MEYER AND RACHEL SALMON ON ELIOT'S READER

[Kinereth Meyer and Rachel Salmon are lecturers in English at Bar-Ilan University in Israel. Both have published several articles on modern poetry. In "The Journey of the Magi," they argue, Eliot engages the reader in the Magus's hesitation and his inability to detach objectively from the details of the recollection.]

T. S. Eliot's 1927 conversion to Anglo-Catholicism changed his relationship with his reading public. Whereas previously readers had been able to identify with the authorial voice, and thus feel a measure of superiority and complacency towards the personae and towards the portrayal of post-World War I spiritual malaise found in the early poems, the later poetry made such complacency impossible. Not only did Eliot begin to speak from a different perspective and with a different voice, he also began to introduce subject matter which would possibly alienate readers immersed in a secular culture. Our purpose here is to examine how Eliot's poetry of conversion overcomes this alienation and draws the reader into speaking the dormant language of tradition. We are interested in the techniques Eliot used in order to put his readers back in touch with "what they feel already," or, alternatively, with "new variations of sensibility which can be appropriated." To read Eliot's poetry in this way is to consider it performatively, that is, to trace its "work" upon the reader.

Written shortly after Eliot's June, 1927, baptism and confirmation in the Anglican Church, "Journey of the Magi" may be read as a model for the way the performative aspects of language function along with the mimetic in Eliot's poetry of conversion. Like the other poems in the *Ariel* series, "Journey of the Magi" gradually undermines its own referentiality. Although the poem begins with the retelling of a well-known New Testament story, the reader soon discovers that the familiar tale has become less, rather than more, accessible; instead of opening itself to recovery by the reader, it engages the reader in its unreadability.

The persona of "Journey of the Magi," apparently himself a Magus, is revealed through the details he recalls, which become for the reader the objective correlatives of his state of mind. Sounding at times like an effete Oriental voluptuary [lines 8–10] and at others like a typical disgruntled tourist [lines 13–15], the Magus seems more like one of the vaguely ridiculous characters of the early poetry than a candidate for a central role in the imminent mystery of the Nativity.

The emphasis here on the visual recollection of experience ("the camel men cursing and grumbling"), or, alternately, on a state of mind *about* experience ("a hard time we had of it"), draws upon techniques, familiar from Romantic memory poems, which appear to sanction the detachment and objectivity of the reader. The last two lines of the first stanza, however, disturb any detachment towards what seems to be the narration of a past event [lines 17–20]. Do these voices speak a language of doubt, implying that the difficult journey to Bethlehem is nothing but folly; or, alternatively, do the voices come from a source beyond the psyche and persist in "singing in our ears" even while "we" grumble discontentedly at our lot? Does the progression of revelation continue, in other words, even if the human participant in the revelation kicks against the invisible chains which seem to tie him to it? The indeterminacy of the voices blocks a univocal mimetic construction and thus puts a performative reading into play, causing the reader to oscillate between the mundane and the miraculous, between doubt and assent.

—Kinereth Meyer and Rachel Salmon, "The Poetry of Conversion as Language Act: Gerard Manley Hopkins and T. S. Eliot," in *Gerard Manley Hopkins and Critical Discourse*, ed. Eugene Hollahan (New York: AMS Press, 1993), 246–7.

JAMES TUTTLETON ON THE CRISIS OF THE MODERN

[James Tuttleton is Professor of English at New York University and the author of *Vital Signs: Essays on American Literature and Criticism* (1996) and *A Fine Silver Thread: Essays on American Writing and Criticism* (1998), from which this extract is taken. Tuttleton cites several of Eliot's essays and letters about his religious beliefs. Eliot's rejection of secular modernism and his conversion to Christianity drew criticism from many of his contemporaries, suggesting that the Magus's sense of alienation parallels Eliot's own: in the poem as in the prose, Eliot addresses the inadequacy of a secular worldview and the "bitterness" of accepting the Incarnation.]

The remarkable reaction in England and America to Eliot's acceptance of the Anglican faith is a vivid indication of how his critique of secular humanism had highlighted the crisis of the modern. For most of his *avant-garde* contemporaries, Eliot's conversion amounted to a betrayal of modernism itself. [...]

Eliot clearly understood that, to his contemporaries, his conversion had the appearance of a "desperate belief." But deep immersion in skeptical thought in modern philosophy, as well as in the texts of the New Humanists, had given him an unshakable conviction that "a Christian world-order, *the* Christian world-order, is ultimately the only one which, from any point of view, will work." He accounted for the final emergence of his faith by a process of "rejection and elimination" very much like that experienced by the skeptic Pascal: "The Christian thinker" finds the world "inexplicable by any non-religious theory: among religions he finds Christianity, and Catholic Christianity, to account most satisfactorily for the world and especially for the moral world within; and thus, by what Newman calls "powerful and concurrent" reasons, he finds himself inexorably committed to the dogma of the Incarnation."

For Eliot, the Christian revelation in the Incarnation was "the only full revelation" and he described "the division between those who accept, and those who deny, Christian revelation . . . to be the most profound division between human beings." For those humanists who diagnosed his conversion as the swallowing of or pretense to belief in "incredible dogma" for the sake of "the luxury of Christian sentiments and the excitement of Christian ritual," Eliot decisively demurred: "For some the process is exactly opposite. Rational assent may arrive late, intellectual conviction may come slowly, but they come inevitably without violence to honesty and nature."

Far from being a luxury, far from constituting a refuge from the ordinary problematics of the ethical life, religion for Eliot

> brought at least the perception of something above morals, and therefore extremely terrifying; it has brought me not happiness, but

the sense of something above happiness and therefore more terrifying than ordinary pain and misery; the very dark night and the desert. To me, the phrase "to be damned for the glory of God" is sense and not paradox; I had far rather walk, as I do, in daily terror of eternity, than feel that this was only a children's game in which all the contestants would get equally worthless prizes in the end.

Religion, finally, gave him a hold on "the tip of the tail of something quite real, more real than morals, or than sweetness and light and culture." That something he defined in "Religion and Literature" as "the primacy of the supernatural over the natural life. . . ."

Although Eliot's conversion cannot be said to have profoundly affected the growth of secular modernism in the West, it had the effect of dramatically identifying the central inadequacy of a merely humanistic view of life. That the most brilliant poet and learned writer of his time should have submitted himself in utter humility to the spiritual authority of the Church called anachronistic by his *avant-garde* contemporaries—highlights the crisis of modernity as perhaps no other event does in the life of a single artist or thinker of this century.

—James Tuttleton, "T. S. Eliot and the Crisis of the Modern," *A Fine Silver Thread: Essays on American Writing and Criticism* (1998) 12, 14–15.

Works by
T. S. Eliot

POETRY

Prufrock and Other Observations
(1917)

Poems (1919)

Ara Vos Prec (1920)

Poems (1920)

The Waste Land (1922)

Poems, 1909–1925 (1925)

Journey of the Magi (1927)

A Song for Simeon (1928)

Animula (1929)

Ash-Wednesday (1930)

Marina (1930)

Triumphal March (1931)

Collected Poems, 1909–1935 (1936)

Old Possum's Book of Practical Cats
(1939)

East Coker (1940)

Burnt Norton (1941)

The Dry Salvages (1941)

Little Gidding (1942)

Four Quartets (1944)

The Complete Poems and Plays,
1909–1950 (1952)

Collected Poems, 1909–1962 (1963)

Poems Written in Early Youth (1967)

The Complete Poems and Plays of T. S.
Eliot (1969)

Inventions of the March Hare: Poems
1909–1917 ed. Christopher Ricks
(1996)

DRAMA

Sweeney Agonistes (1932)

The Rock (1934)

Murder in the Cathedral (1935)

The Family Reunion (1939)

The Cocktail Party (1950)

The Confidential Clerk (1954)

The Elder Statesman (1959)

Collected Plays (1962)

ESSAYS

Ezra Pound, His Metric and His Poetry
(1918)

The Sacred Wood (1920)

Homage to John Dryden (1924)

For Lancelot Andrewes (1928)

Dante (1929)

Thoughts after Lambeth (1931)

Selected Essays 1917–1932 (1932)

John Dryden: The Poet, the Dramatist,
the Critic (1932)

The Use of Poetry and the Use of Criticism (1933)

After Strange Gods (1934)

Elizabethan Essays (1934)

Essays Ancient and Modern (1936)

The Idea of a Christian Society (1939)

Notes Towards the Definition of Culture
(1948)

On Poetry and Poets (1957)

George Herbert (1962)

Knowledge and Experience in the Philosophy of F. H. Bradley (1964)

To Criticize the Critic, and other writings (1965)

Selected Prose of T. S. Eliot ed. Frank
Kermode (1975)

Works about
T. S. Eliot

Ackroyd, Peter. *T. S. Eliot: A Life*. New York: Simon and Schuster, 1984.

Allan, Mowbray. *T. S. Eliot's Impersonal Theory of Poetry*. Lewisburg, PA: Bucknell University Press, 1974.

Antrim, Harry T. *T. S. Eliot's Concept of Language*. Gainsville, FL: University of Florida Humanities Monographs, 1971.

Basu, Tapan Kumar, ed. *T. S. Eliot: An Anthology of Recent Criticism*. Delhi: Pencraft International: 1993.

Bedient, Calvin. *He Do the Police in Different Voices: The Waste Land and its Protagonist*. Chicago: University of Chicago Press, 1986.

Beehler, Michael. *T. S. Eliot, Wallace Stevens, and the Discourses of Difference*. Baton Rouge: Louisiana State University Press, 1987.

Bergonzi, Bernard. *T. S. Eliot*. New York: Macmillan, 1972.

Bloom, Harold, ed. *T. S. Eliot's The Waste Land*. New York: Chelsea House, 1986.

Bolgan, Anne C. *What the Thunder Really Said: A Retrospective Essay on the Making of The Waste Land*. Montreal: McGill-Queen's University Press, 1973.

Brooker, Jewel Spears. *Mastery and Escape: T. S. Eliot and the Dialectic of Modernism*. Amherst: University of Massachusetts Press, 1994.

Bush, Ronald. *T. S. Eliot: A Study in Character and Style*. New York: Oxford University Press, 1983.

Christ, Carol T. "T. S. Eliot and the Victorians." *Modern Philology* (November 1981): 157–65.

Clarke, Graham, ed. *T. S. Eliot: Critical Assessments*. London: Christopher Helm, 1990. 4 vols.

Cook, Eleanor. "T. S. Eliot and the Carthaginian Peace." *ELH* 46 (1979): 341–55.

Cookson, Linda and Bryan Loughrey, eds. *Critical Essays on The Waste Land*. Harlow: Longmans, 1988.

Donker, Marjorie. "*The Waste Land* and the *Aeneid*." *PMLA* 89 (1974): 164–71.

Eliot, Valerie, ed. *The Waste Land: A Facsimile and Transcript of the Original Drafts, Including the Annotations of Ezra Pound.* New York: Harcourt Brace Jovanovich, 1971.

Everett, Barbara. "Eliot's Marianne: *The Waste Land* and Its Poetry of Europe." *The Review of English Studies* 31, no. 121 (1980): 41–53.

Frye, Northrop. *T. S. Eliot.* New York: Capricorn Books, 1963.

Gallup, Donald. T. S. Eliot: A Bibliography. Rev. ed. New York: Harcourt Brace Jovanovich, 1969.

Gardner, Helen. *The Art of T. S. Eliot.* New York: Dutton, 1950.

Gish, Nancy K. *The Waste Land: A Poem of Memory and Desire.* Boston: Twayne, 1988.

Grant, Michael, ed. *T. S. Eliot: The Critical Heritage.* 2 vols. London: Routledge and Kegan Paul, 1982.

Hough, Graham. *Reflections on a Literary Revolution.* Washington, DC: The Catholic University of America Press, 1960.

Jay, Gregory. *T. S. Eliot and the Poetics of Literary History.* Baton Rouge: Louisiana State University Press, 1983.

Litz, A. Walton, ed. *Eliot in His Time: Essays on the Occasion of the Fiftieth Anniversary of The Waste Land.* Princeton: Princeton University Press, 1973.

Kenner, Hugh. *The Invisible Poet: T. S. Eliot.* London: W. H. Allen, 1960.

————, ed. *T. S. Eliot: A Collection of Critical Essays.* Englewood Cliffs, NJ: Prentice-Hall, 1965.

Kermode, Frank, ed. *Selected Prose of T. S. Eliot.* London: Faber and Faber, 1975.

Kojecky, Roger. *T. S. Eliot's Social Criticism.* New York: Farrar, Straus and Giroux, 1971.

Manganiello, Dominic. *T. S. Eliot and Dante.* New York: St. Martin's Press, 1989.

Matthiessen, F. O. *The Achievement of T. S. Eliot: An Essay on the Nature of Poetry.* New York: Oxford University Press, 1947.

Nevo, Ruth. "The Waste Land: Ur-Text of Deconstruction." *New Literary History* 13 (Spring 1982): 95–102.

North, Michael. The Political Aesthetic of Yeats, Eliot, and Pound. Cambridge: Cambridge University Press, 1991.

Olney, James, ed. *T. S. Eliot: Essays from the Southern Review*. Oxford: Oxford University Press, 1988.

Phillips, Caroline. *Religious Quest in the Poetry of T. S. Eliot*. Lewiston: Edwin Mellen, 1995.

Pinkney, Tony. *Women in the Poetry of T. S. Eliot: A Psychoanalytic Approach*. London: Macmillan, 1984.

Ricks, Christopher. *T. S. Eliot and Prejudice*. London: Faber, 1988.

Southam, B. C. *A Student's Guide to the Selected Poems of T. S. Eliot*. Boston: Faber and Faber, 1990.

Smith, Grover. *T. S. Eliot's Poetry and Plays: A Study in Sources and Meaning*. Chicago: The University of Chicago Press, 1956.

_____. *The Waste Land*. London: Allen & Unwin, 1983.

Tamplin, Ronald. *A Preface to T. S. Eliot*. New York: Longman, 1987.

Tate, Allen, ed. *T. S. Eliot: The Man and his Work*. New York: Delacorte Press, 1966.

Unger, Leonard. *T. S. Eliot: Moments and Patterns*. Minneapolis: University of Minnesota Press, 1961.

_____, ed. *T. S. Eliot: A Selected Critique*. New York: Russell & Russell, 1966.

Ward, David. *T. S. Eliot Between Two Worlds: A Reading of T. S. Eliot's Poetry and Plays*. Boston: Routledge & Kegan Paul, 1973.

Williamson, George. *A Reader's Guide to T. S. Eliot: A Poem-by-Poem Analysis*. New York: Farrar, Straus & Giroux, 1966.

Index of
Themes and Ideas